# CROSSCURRENTS

VOLUME 69, NO 3 ISSN 0011-1953


## GUILT AND IMPURITY

**Edited by Katharina von Kellenbach**

**235**
*Introduction*
**Katharina von Kellenbach**

**238**
*Guilt and Its Purification: The Church and Sexual Abuse*
**Katharina von Kellenbach**

**252**
*Weeds Among the Wheat: The Impurity of the Church Between Tolerance, Solace, and Guilt Denial*
**Meinolf Schumacher**

**264**
*Purity and Kashrut*
**Deborah Williger**

**277**
*"Clean" Collections: On the Idea of Contamination in the Provenance Discussion*
**Roger Fayet**

**291**
*Shit Bucket Campaigns and Nestbeschmutzer: The Waldheim Affair in Austria*
**Iris Hermann**

**301**
*Purifying Indonesia, Purifying Women: The National Commission for Women's Rights and the 1965-1968 Anti-Communist Violence*
**Nelly van Doorn-Harder**

**319**
*The Bible's Greatest Meme?*
**Peter Heinegg**

**323**
*Condemning the Congregation*
**Peter Heinegg**

**328**
*Summa Anti-Theologica*
**Peter Heinegg**

**334**
*Disfellowshipped!*
**Peter Heinegg**

**337**
*John V. Tolan*
**Peter Heinegg**

**341**
*Notes on Contributors*

About the Cover: The cover photo was taken by Stefan Adamick.

***CrossCurrents*** (ISSN 0011-1953; online ISSN 1939-3881) connects the wisdom of the heart with the life of the mind and the experiences of the body. The journal is operated through its parent organization, the Association for Public Religion and Intellectual Life (APRIL), an interreligious network of academics, activists, artists, and community leaders seeking to engage the many ways religion meets the public. Contributions to the journal exist at the nexus of religion, education, the arts, and social justice. The journal is published quarterly on behalf of the Association for Public Religion and Intellectual Life by the University of North Carolina Press.

The Association for Public Religion and Intellectual Life (formerly ARIL) is a global network of leaders, scholars, and social change agents who explore religious life, engage in intellectual inquiry, and lead ethical action in the world today. Their primary objective, especially through annual summer colloquia and *CrossCurrents*, is to bring together leading voices of our time to advocate for justice and to examine global spiritual and interreligious currents in both historical and contemporary perspectives.

A membership to APRIL includes access to *CrossCurrents* starting with Volume 58, 2008, though our partners at Project MUSE, monthly newsletters, early access to summer colloquium themes, a 40% on UNC Press books, and more. For more information, including membership and subscription rates, visit www.aprilonline.org.

This reissue of *CrossCurrents* was one of four issues published in 2019 as part of Volume 69. For a current masthead visit www.aprilonline.org.



ISBN 978-1-4696-6720-1 (Print)

# INTRODUCTION

Metaphors of purity and impurity surface in different contexts and mean wildly different things depending on their moral, aesthetic, political, and ritual frame of reference. Jewish ritual food laws use categories of pure and impure that were put to very different use in Nazi campaigns to purify Germany of degenerate art and polluted blood, a rhetoric that reemerges in present debates over looted and stolen works of art that threaten to "contaminate" museum collections. Visions of purity and practices of purification resist normative definition, but the language of "dirty hands" and "white vests," "money laundering" and "dirt bags" signals the strong association of aesthetic and moral categories.

"Dirt is what we find dirty, more or less" writes Colin McGinn in his book on *Disgust,* noting that "there is no natural kind of dirt."[1] Indeed, as Mary Douglas famously pointed out, dirt refers to anything that is considered "out of place."[2] Dirt is not defined by any essence or substance but rather by its placement within systems of meaning. The location and dislocation of objects, people, and ideas are not emotionally neutral experiences, but trigger intense feelings of either disgust or delight. Purity, clarity, and harmony make us happy, while chaos, slime, and disorder cause us distress. Consider the difference that context makes: Food on a dinner plate is delicious and enticing, but food that dropped to the floor or into the garbage bin turns revolting and horrid. Placement and displacement are linked to emotional states of revulsion or satisfaction. This makes appeals to purity and purification so powerful and effective to mobilize political campaigns. The portrayal of Jews as creepy vermin and dangerous pollution made ethnic cleansing and genocide appear reasonable and acceptable. In the aftermath, the guilty remainders and reminders of Nazi rule disturbed the symbolic and political order of peaceful democratic, post-war Europe. Guilt, like dirt, must be hidden and buried, removed, and wiped away.

Purity discourses are not a uniquely conservative phenomenon, although sexual purity, ethnic integrity, and national borders are peculiar desires of a conservative imaginary. Progressives denounce sexual predation and political incorrectness with purgatory passion. The Church hierarchy's tolerance of sexual and criminal misconduct among its clergy intensified furious calls for comprehensive purification. The expulsion of wrongdoers (out of the community and into prison, exile, and oblivion) promises to purify, renew, and reform. Purification always involves violence, as order is created or restored by elimination and destruction. Indonesia established its "New Order" in 1966 by killing up to one million Indonesians suspected of being communists and defiling alleged communist women by systematically raping them. Now, these women who lived in a state of impurity for decades begin to reclaim and reverse the discourse of purity and impurity. Visions of purity fuel genocidal campaigns and the politics of ethnic cleansing, but they also inform movements that demand reparation, redress, and accountability. There is no objective platform, from which one could judge the correct and the incorrect use of these metaphors. Andrew Brower Latz argues in "Purity in Future Theology" that the "use of the concept of purity as a social or political category is a theoretical and practical mistake because it evades fundamental ambiguities and encourages authoritarianism and distorted forms of morality."[3] He rejects any future use in theology as well, since these concepts are intrinsically tied to "genocide, fundamentalism, simplistic attitudes to sex, and dangerous and/or simplistic attitudes to cultural and group identities."[4] But will we be able to "purge" purity from our language, politics, and aesthetics? Its very slipperiness, I would argue, makes this metaphor appealing, as it is constantly being revised. Certainly, any time, it is taken literally and absolutized, people suffer the destructive consequences of purification.

In this volume, we explore various rhetorical uses of purity and impurity. The authors convened for a conference on Purity and Impurity in March 2019 at the Center for Interdisciplinary Research (ZiF) of the Bielefeld University, Germany. Several lectures were delivered in German, and we are greatly indebted to Peter Heinegg who quickly and skillfully translated the original German into English. The ZiF was founded fifty years ago to support international interdisciplinary research. It funds interdisciplinary research groups that convene for ten months in Bielefeld to pursue a common scholarly project. Several of the authors are fellows of the ZIF Research Group "Felix Culpa: Guilt as a Culturally Productive Force." We have explored the culturally irritating and productive presence of guilt in literature, psychology, history, law, religion, and politics over the course of 2018–2019. Several international conferences brought additional guests to the ZiF in order to broaden and deepen our discussions. This volume brings together scholars from art history, medieval literature, veterinary medicine and Jewish studies, as well as Islamic and religious studies. We hope it will give insight into the diversity of perspectives on the rhetoric of purity and impurity as that intersects with guilt.

**Notes**

1. Colin McGinn, *The Meaning of Disgust*. New York: Oxford University Press, 2011, 31.
2. Mary Douglas, *Purity and Danger: An Analysis of Concepts of Pollution and Taboo*. London and Henley: Routledge & Kegan Paul, 1966.
3. Andrew Brower Latz, "Purity in Future Theology," In *Purity: Essays in Bible and Theology*, edited by Andrew Brower Latz and Arseny Ermakov, Eugene, OR: Wipf and Stock Publishers, 250.
4. Andrew Brower Latz, "Purity in Future Theology," p. 260.

*—Katharina von Kellenbach*

# GUILT AND ITS PURIFICATION

## The Church and Sexual Abuse

**Katharina von Kellenbach**

Amidst the horror of ongoing revelations about the Roman Catholic Church's complicity in sexual predation, a theological reflection on Christian teachings about guilt and reconciliation is enlightening. Flawed notions of Christian forgiveness have brought us to this point where priests are absolved of crimes by their colleagues and reassigned to different posts in blind faith in their resolve to begin anew. The mystery of redemption is at the heart of the Christian message, which makes this systemic failure sadly predictable and particularly painful. What is wrong with the Christian theory and practice of sin and forgiveness that it fails to resist devastating complicity? Shifting focus from redemption to guilt invites reflection on the problematic metaphors that facilitate quick release and premature closure. The language of guilt invokes the imagery of stains and impurities that must be purified (by the sacrificial blood of Christ) or of burdens and weights that can be lifted and carried away (by a substitutionary scapegoat). In either case, guilt disappears as if by magic. This essay questions this imagery and draws on ecologically informed, sustainable practices of purification in order to propose a sequence of ritual steps to transform personal and collective guilt in the wake of the sexual abuse crisis.

We rarely stop to define guilt, because it is immediately linked to forgiveness. Guilt and forgiveness, sin and redemption are paired concepts that are mentioned in the same breath. But what is guilt? Is it an individual feeling or an objective condition? The term is often used interchangeably, although the emotion and the state of being guilty are, unfortunately, very different experiences. In fact, it is one of the cruel ironies that victims *feel* guilty, while perpetrators remain indifferent to and oblivious about the harm they caused. It is the victims who are wracked by guilt feelings, sometimes severely so. Depression, anxiety, trouble sleeping, and nightmares are common experiences among survivors. The symptom of survivor guilt would eventually be incorporated into the emerging concept of "trauma" and its official clinical diagnosis as PTSD, post-traumatic stress syndrome.[1] Among its four symptoms, listed by National Institute of Health, are "distorted feelings like guilt or blame" and "negative thoughts about oneself or the world."[2] Much of the psychoanalytic discourse on guilt is victim-centered since research is driven by patients who consult psychoanalysts and psychotherapists.[3] And it is the victims of traumatic violence who are plagued by intense emotions of guilt, rage, shame, and powerlessness. Perpetrators rarely consult therapists, counselors, or confessors. As long as perpetrators do not present with symptoms or are required by law to sign up for therapy [as pedophiles and sex offenders must do according to German law],[4] there are few empirical studies on the symptomology of a "perpetrator syndrome." The diagnosis of "post-traumatic stress syndrome" describes the experience of victims rather than perpetrators.

Martin Buber insisted on the difference between "real" or "ontic" guilt and guilt feelings in a lecture at a Conference on Medical Psychotherapy in 1948, which was subsequently published as "Guilt and Guilt Feelings."[5] A therapist, Buber warned, should not ignore the "external life of his patient and especially the actions and attitudes therein, and again especially the patient's active share in the manifold relation between him and the human world."[6] There is a difference, Buber argued, between the emotional (neurotic) response and the actual violation of the order of being (*Seinsordnung*). Guilt and guilt feelings are inversely related: Perpetrators lack feelings of guilt, while victims are wracked by self-blame, shame, and guilt feelings.

The symptoms of guilt manifest as lack of empathy, an absence of sensitivity, an obstruction of moral response to the suffering of others.[7] To harm another requires a barrier that shields against responsiveness to suffering. Every act of violence involves a hardening of the heart, to use the Biblical concept, on the part of the perpetrator. We will leave aside the theological question of ultimate responsibility and whether it is "The

LORD [who] hardened Pharaoh's heart" (Ex 10:20; 10:27, 11:10; 14:8; Jos 11:20). Psychologically, denial is cause and effect of harming another being. It is intrinsic to the infliction of harm. "He has blinded their eyes, and hardened their heart, so that they might not look with their eyes and understand with their heart" (John 12:40). Perpetrators avert their eyes and block their ears to avoid seeing, feeling, and hearing the pain inflicted on victims. This is true for all acts of violence, but especially so for agents who act within structures of authority that use legitimate force to maintain order. Hierarchical systems give some people power over others who are deemed essentially different and in need of control because of some perceived lack of rationality, authority, or agency. Ideologies of gender, sexuality, age, ability, race, and class justify why certain people deserve less protection of their integrity and autonomy and somehow feel less pain and suffering. As long as such ideological force fields remain operative, there is no consciousness of culpable wrongdoing. Atrocities, which on Claudia Card's definition include sexual and domestic violence against women and children, suck entire communities into moral indifference, complicity, and denial.[8]

If the dis-ease consists in the absence of cognitive and emotional guilt awareness, then the cure cannot rightly promise release from its burden or purification of its remainders. But this is exactly what the liturgical and sacramental language of reconciliation promises. Built on biblical models of sacrificial atonement, Christ's death saves because his blood washes away sin and because he bears the weight of iniquity. Such metaphors are invoked to explain his death for the "forgiveness of our trespasses" (Eph 2:13), "that he might redeem us from all iniquity and purify for himself a people of his own who are zealous for good deeds" (Titus 2:14). In the sacraments of baptism, "you were washed, you were sanctified, you were justified" (1 Cor 6:11) and of the eucharist, where the "blood of Jesus Christ his Son cleanses us from all sin" (1 John 1:7). This language is not unique to Christianity.[9] Sacrificial blood and sacred water are universal detergents to cleanse spiritual and social violations of the social and symbolic order. In the Hebrew Bible, trespasses against God's divine ordinances require expiation that take the form of rituals of purification, often involving the entire community, which is mandated to purify in response to violation of the sacred law. Unless the culprit is punished, the entire community is implicated in guilt by association, which pollutes the land, undermines social cohesion, and obstructs relations with G-d:

> You shall not pollute the land in which you live; for the blood pollutes the land, and no expiation can be made for the land, for the blood that is shed in it, except by the blood of the one who shed it. You shall not defile the land in which you live, in which I dwell; for I the LORD dwell among the Israelites. (Num 35:33–34)

On the Biblical paradigm, it is the entire community that is implicated and under obligation to respond, prosecute, and punish the culprit. Only some people in a community are guilty, but all are responsible. Unless and until a community vindicates the victims by imposing the rule of law, the pollution of moral violation spreads.[10] While this may sound like an ancient tribal blood feud custom, we can see this dynamic clearly playing out in the current church crisis, which stems from the community's failure to mark wrong and punish wrongdoing. The cover-up becomes the pollution, in addition and quite distinct from the original crime of sexual predation. Retribution checks this contamination and restores moral health to the community.[11] The scapegoat ritual provides the other setting by which a community rids itself of personal and communal guilt:

> Then Aaron shall lay both his hands on the head of the live goat, and confess over it all the iniquities of the people of Israel, and all their transgressions, all their sins, putting them on the head of the goat, and sending it away into the wilderness by means of someone designated for the task. The goat shall bear on itself all their iniquities to a barren region; and the goat shall be set free in the wilderness. (Lev 16:20–22)

This ritual visualizes sin and guilt as a burden that can be loaded and carried away. In Christianity, Christ takes on the role of sacrificial substitute who carries away the weight of iniquity and disposes it somewhere safely in a remote corner of the universe. This language must be challenged on moral and ecological grounds: The remainders of wrongdoing do not disappear magically, and they do not drain down mysterious pipes or vanish on the backs of waste management scapegoats. But these metaphors are suggestive and can be used to imagine new approaches to guilt contagion by association. A toxic pile radiates, pollutes, and contaminates. Guilt accrues as a result of a community's inability and unwillingness to censure evil and does not magically evaporate. It must be cleaned-up, bioremediated, and composted.

The metaphor of composting affirms the messy materiality of the past and enriches existing imagery of washing and waste removal. Composting the remainders of wrongdoing requires patience and engagement, strategy and supervision. The etymology of the word is derived from the Latin *compositum* (later *compostum*) which the OED defines as "(1) composition, combination, compound, (2) literary composition, compendium, as well as (3) a mixture of various ingredients for fertilizing or enriching land, a prepared manure or mould."[12] It is the exact opposite of purity, which is defined as "the state or quality of being free from extraneous or foreign elements, or from outside influence; the state of being unadulterated or refined." Purity is white and clear, immaculate and untouched, while compost is rich, dark, smelly, and blended. When Pope John Paull II spoke of the "purification of memory" to guide the millennial celebrations in 2000, he invited the Church to come to terms with history, including the crusades, the inquisition, the slave trade, colonialism, and the Holocaust.[13] He invoked the image of the Virgin Mary, whose purity consists of youth, innocence, and intactness. The old is never innocent, and that is true for individuals as much as for religious heritages and national histories. Age, inevitably, accumulates breakage and malfunction, failure and debris. By envisioning purity in the image of the Virgin, the untouched bride, "dressed in a simple robe of white linen, the finest linen, bright and pure"[14] we scorn processes of maturation and ripening. By contrast, symbols such as fermented wine or leavened bread could be used to appreciate processes of fermentation and aging. Wine gets better with age. Sour dough enlivens tasteless and bland flour into flavorful bread. Purity that derives from composting validates the digestion of the old, broken, discarded, and the guilty into rich, new ground for being.

Even the most poisonous remainders can be digested into basic stable elements. Scientists have only recently begun to use composting for the most protracted cases, known as POC (persistent organic compounds) that resist natural biological degradation. Bioremediation proves promising and often successful. But even if it did not, what else, exactly, is supposed to happen to toxic garbage, including radioactive waste? Neither our material garbage nor our moral legacies dissolve into thin air. Composting sequesters detritus but does not pretend its magic elimination. The new always grows out of the old. Putrefaction and fermentation create the conditions in which the new takes root and grows.

The Catholic Church has a sacramental system of penance that lends itself to sustainable practices of critical engagement with past wrongdoing. Its performative sacramental process prescribes three distinct steps before absolution. This sacrament aims at spiritual reconciliation with God and is facilitated by an ordained priest, but its basic grammar is applicable to any process of repair of relationship and recovery of personal integrity. The three steps are: *contritio cordis*, heartfelt contrition, *confessio oris*, verbal confession, and *satisfactio operis,* acts of penitential restitution. They are self-explanatory. The most secular people expect culprits to show some remorse, to admit their wrongdoing, and to repair the damage as much as possible. These are the cues that people are looking for, for instance, when we watch prominent men who have been accused by the #MeToo movement apologize and attempt to return to public life. In private and public, we decide, based on the performance of these steps, whether we are willing to grant forgiveness.

What makes the language of sacraments intriguing is precisely their performative, external character. Sacraments are “outward and visible signs of an inward and invisible grace.” This makes them relevant to the real world, where actions count. It is the visible performance of penance that establishes credibility and integrity more so than the internal changes to the soul. Of course, Martin Luther was right to observe that the depth and quality of a person’s contrition can never be measured or proven. Every apology is a performance, which may or may not be heartfelt. Luther concluded from this fact that contrition should not be made the condition of God’s grace and justification. On his view, contrition is the gift of justification, which is received unconditionally and works to open the eyes and soften the heart. Penance and sanctification follow after this change of heart has occurred. God’s unconditional justification works to convert the sinner and to generate internal feelings of remorse and contrition.

Luther was right that contrition is a precious gift. The evidence that contrition is lacking and woefully incomplete is overwhelming. We certainly also observe that in the case of the Roman Catholic hierarchy. Just the other week, retired Pope Benedict XVI issued a statement blaming the "scandal of sexual abuse" on secular culture, declining faith in God, and resistance to the doctrinal authority of the church. His rambling letter left open the possibility that the scandal was caused by the audacity and insolence of the victims rather than the moral bankruptcy of the leadership. Pope Benedict XVI, who has controlled the highest levers of power in the Church for decades, does not feel any remorse. In his view, the injured party is the Church (and he himself) rather than the victims of clergy sexual abuse, who are barely mentioned. He does not apologize.[15]

How does one purify recalcitrance? Conversions do not happen instantaneously. They require time and active engagement, which makes the metaphor of composting apt and compelling. The Roman Catholic sacrament mandates a threefold engagement with wrongdoing: *Contritio cordis* cultivates intellectual recognition and moral knowledge of what has happened; *confessio oris* exacts transparency and seeks language that can convey the truth of events that are unimaginable and indescribable; *satisfactio operis* implements reparative action to recompense the victims and to work toward institutional change of the conditions that enabled the wrongdoing. This process is not chronological or sequential, there is no beginning, middle, and end. It is an interlocking spiral that is cumulative and transformative.

## *Contritio Cordis: rituals of repudiation*

Contrition must be cultivated in rituals of repudiation, in which and through which communities mark wrongdoing. Rituals of repudiation are speech acts that take the form of, for instance, apologies, court room trials, and removal from power and authority. They are symbolic and exemplary and signal a community's normative negotiations over the boundaries of right and wrong. Without such rituals of condemnation, contrition does not emerge. As Paul Ricoeur pointed out in *The Symbolism of Evil,* evil "is not a taint that exists absolutely without reference to a field of human presence, to words that express defilement. A man is defiled in the sight of certain men, in the language of certain men. Only he is defiled who is regarded as defiled; a law is required to say it; the interdict is itself a defining utterance ... This 'education' of the feeling of impurity by the language which defines and legislates is of capital importance."[16] As long as a community fails to mark the boundaries of good and evil, contrition does not emerge. As long as perpetrators, such as Cardinal McCarrick of Washington, DC, whose coercive escapades with seminarians had long been known, ascended through the ranks of power, there was no contrition. Apologies, criminal prosecution, and loss of power and authority create the preconditions for experiences of contrition.[17]

Apologies have become routinized.[18] Words are cheap. But they still do not come easy. Apologies are contested, demanded, delivered, debated, rejected, or accepted. When a Pope (or head of state, or CEO) issues a formal apology on behalf of an institution, they signal a community's disavowal of practices, policies, and persons that were previously tolerated. Public apologies accept personal and institutional responsibility and denounce particular behaviors. Apologies remain controversial, and we can all think of instances, where apologies were refused or delivered halfheartedly. Successful aologies are not singular events, but are repeated. Germany, for instance, is routinely delivering apologies, when invited to commemorations, while Japan seems to assume, falsely, that one apology should suffice.[19] To work as ritual events, apologies must be repeated and become better, more precise, and factually more accurate over time. The precision, veracity, and integrity of apologies provide a fairly precise measure of the degree of change after wrongdoing.

Court proceedings are another ritual of repudiation. Of course, it is usually only a few exemplary offenders who are brought to justice and subjected to the drama of indictment and defense, deliberation, and sentencing. The majority of criminals, in all societies, get away. But some are caught, prosecuted, and declared guilty. Their punishment follows a finely grained system of codes that mark the severity of the offense in the currency of pain and harm. The worse the offense the harsher the penalty. In the contemporary world, most societies measure crime in prison time. But historically, there have been other methods involving physical harm or financial compensation for lost eyes, teeth, limbs, and life. Punishments have always been symbolic forms of marking and renouncing wrongdoing and criminality. Over the course of history, communities have experimented with exile and expulsion, physical punishments, monetary restitution, stigmatization and enslavement. Modern Western societies seem to have settled on incarceration. This may require rethinking and revision. But while we may need to reconsider the nature of punitive pain in light of the crisis of mass incarceration, we cannot forego punishments altogether without risking communal complicity. Bishops may not need to go to prison, but their impunity signals lack of respect for victims. Punishments express a community's normative values that determine whose lives matter, who deserves protection, and whose voice shall be heard.

Rape, incest, and the sexual abuse of children *have always been prohibited.* But, despite universal criminalization, victims find it exceedingly hard to speak, to find support, to seek justice, and to move communities to sanction their tormenters. Even in war zones, victims of political and military mass rape know to remain silent. They cannot trust their own families to take their side over the side of their torturers. No victim of a Catholic priest could ever assume that their family, their teachers, their counselors, or the police would believe them.[20] The sexual exploitation of women and children is not a minor failure or marginal flaw but intrinsic to patriarchal organizations that prescribe silence and submission as the divinely ordained vocation of women and children. Vulnerability is compounded by invisibility and powerlessness. The "scandal of sexual abuse," which has gathered steam over the last twenty years, is the result of the cultural empowerment of women and children. For the most part, the Church hierarchy has resisted these changes and conspired to silence its most vulnerable and weak members.

Rituals of repudiation, in the form of apologies, court trials, and resignations, shift the discursive field. They also purge institutions in instrumental ways. The entire structure of an all-male, celibate hierarchy (Greek: *hieros-archy* = sacred rule of priests) is at stake. Contrition involves more than recognition of individual failure and exemplary resignations to reconsider the power arrangements that have shaped distorted interactions between clergy and laity, men and women. Nobody knows, at this point in time, what new orders will emerge from this composting approach to the sexual abuse crisis. But this metaphor communicates a strong sense of hope that something *will* sprout from the toxic trauma of guilt. The recognition of fault *will* lead to new insights and perspectives. The community *will* learn to see with new eyes and hear with different ears.

## *Confessio Oris: rituals of transparency*

The shock of the brazen lies of the Roman Catholic hierarchy that calmly denied knowledge of sexual abuse for decades all the while frantically protecting its perpetrators from exposure, dismissal, and prosecution is only slowly sinking in. It has taken the tenacity of victims and their organizations, the detective work of investigative journalists, and the prosecutorial methods of state's attorneys' offices to break through the walls of denial. Now that these walls have been breached, academic research can begin, psychologists can survey and collect data, prepare statistical analysis and psychological theories. What are the causes and conditions of abuse, the scope and solutions? We have no idea. How long has this been going on? We do not know. The archives remain closed. Historians have not (yet) been given access to the files. As an institution, the Church resists requests for information as strenuously as any recalcitrant teenager. Why is a religion that professes faith in Christian reconciliation on the basis of contrition, confession, and satisfaction so utterly opposed to any and all of it?

It is, of course, exceedingly hard to put our most shameful and traumatic secrets into words. While not all religions practice confession, all religions value truth and truthfulness as signs of integrity and purity. In the Jewish and Christian traditions, confession is mandatory for *teshuvah* and repentance. While there is no mediating priest in the Jewish tradition, Maimonides interpreted the commandment in Leviticus 5:5 that "he shall confess the sin he has committed upon" the sacrificial sin offering at the altar, to make confession mandatory. Otherwise, he argued, "unspoken matters that remain in the heart are not significant matters" (Kiddushin 49b). The verbal articulation turns secret acts into real and actionable events. Confessions can be public or private, before God or a priest, communal or individual. The mandate for language and the quest for the truth is rooted in the insight that wrongdoing creates blind spots. Guilt shades the truth and thick layers of deception prevent its exposure.

The truth about sexuality is notoriously elusive. Human civilizations seem to swing between puritanism and promiscuity, double standards and moral panics. And yet, we will need truthful stories to create narratives that can write new laws, create new support structures, and invent new procedures that help people live embodied and sexual lives. How do we speak about sexuality and its violation? Which words will children use, how will women reclaim sexual agency, and perpetrators wrestle with their desires? What constitutes rape culture? How do we define the problem: male sexuality, homosexuality, pedophilia? Violence, assault, submission? Celibacy and abstinence? Consent, seduction, coercion? Speaking truthfully about sexuality has never been an easy task. Despite confession fatigue, we cannot leave it to the professional experts, the confessors and therapists, researchers and historians to define appropriate sexual conduct. We need the entire community, with its artists and musicians, poets and prostitutes to engage in truthful dialogue. That the truth will make us free, is a statement of faith that is more easily professed than practiced in embodied and institutionalized ways.

## *Satisfactio Operis: rituals of penitential restitution*

Punishment, penance, and penitence have become problematic. In the mainline churches, including Roman Catholicism, the God of forgiveness, love, and mercy is emphasized. The God of wrath and revenge, who used to consign sinners to eternal hellfire or to temporary purgatory torture has fallen out of fashion. Liberal Christianity has become tolerant and conciliatory, and nothing seems unforgiveable to this God. Christians see themselves as peaceful and are exhorted to forgive their trespassers seven times seventy times (Mt 18:22). This abandons victims of atrocity who are denied retribution and vindication. The desire to see perpetrator *suffer* the consequences becomes immoral. The Latin word *poena* means pain, punishment, penalty and is derived from the Greek term *poinḗ* (ποινή) meaning blood money, fine, penalty, and punishment. Of course, the line between punishment and abuse has always been exceedingly thin, and the historical experience of religious practices of flagellation and hair shirts, starvation and indulgences are not reassuring. Neither is the current state of the sprawling prison industrial complex. Penitential suffering could be a pointless exercise in cruelty.

Traditionally, the Church imposed penitential works of *satisfactio operis* alongside and in addition to retributive justice delivered by the "sword" of the state. Penances involved prayer and austerities, such as fasting, charity, abstinence, self-mortification, and self-denial and aimed at atonement and reconciliation. Restorative justice theorist Robin Antony Duff is intrigued by penitential practices because they seek to reform and reintegrate perpetrators into the community.[21] Penances are pre-emptive and seek to avoid permanent exclusion by excommunication, exile, and execution. But penances are painful and deprive a person of status, honor, freedom, and money. Hard treatment, writes Duff is a structured exercise that aims to focus a "sinner's attention on his sin and its implication."[22] Suffering, argues orthodox Jewish philosopher Dov Soloveitchik, is the "currency in which the sinner pays the Almighty to regain ownership over himself after he repents."[23] Suffering redeems, changes, transforms. In modern secular socities, this link is no longer self-evident.

But there are other contexts, in which modern secularists accept physical suffering as productive and meaningful. Consider the difference between the physical pain of torture and the physical pain of extreme sports. One form is undertaken voluntarily, the other is inflicted against one's will, for different reasons and with different outcomes. While the physical pain itself may be similar, its meaning is different: Torture is debilitating and disempowering, while climbing Mount Everest is empowering and exhilarating. Penitential suffering should be compared more to hiking in the Himalayan mountains than to torture. Its torment is ennobling and ultimately rewarding. The difference is decisive and elusive, as any educator who penalizes bad behaviors, knows. One easily slips into the other.

What kinds of suffering could members of the Roman Catholic hierarchy undertake to channel retributive rage into reparative action that renews dignity and respect? A fast day for the entire Roman Catholic clergy? A public relinquishment of Church treasure to support the wellbeing of victims? A month of sackcloth for bishops? A vow of silence on matters of controlling the sexual lives of others? A day of remembrance to respect victims and survivors? The Pope crossing the Alps barefoot, as King Heinrich IV did from Germany to Canossa in 1076 to ask for forgiveness? There is actually little public appetite for such symbolic acts of degradation. But we should not discount their potential to preempt anger and to firm up resolve to engage in meaningful action. There is rich repertoire of penitential affliction that transforms silent, speechless shame into active obligation to reach out and serve. Rites of affliction cultivate contrition, elicit respect, and (re)generate trust. Rituals of penitential restitution include financial settlements, charity, and support for survivor organizations; administrative reform, the removal of implicated religious elites, education about sexuality, empowerment of women and children, dialogue, as well as commemorative events to honoro victims.

The call to "clean house" and purify the church easily means "white-washing" or, worse, "sweeping the dirt under the rug." Sending predator priests into retirement (finally) and demoting their complicit supervisors, while huge, will not suffice. Guilt and the guilty do not magically disappear. Guilt must be decontaminated, remediated, composted in cycles of sustainable intervention and transformative strategies. It becomes the ferment that turns the refuse into new ground. Composting provides a productive and hopeful metaphor for purification, because it requires more than washing away the guilt. Instead, it approaches guilt as ferment and leaven that transforms the raw material of failure into life-giving wine and bread. Unless the patriarchal and feudal power arrangements that created the conditions for sexual abuse are decontaminated, fermented, and transformed, these wounds will fester.

**Notes**

1. Leys, Ruth, *From Guilt to Shame: Auschwitz and After* (Princeton: Princeton University Press, 2007).
2. Leys, Ruth, *Trauma: A Genealogy* (Chicago: Chicago University Press, 2000). https://www.nimh.nih.gov/health/topics/post-traumatic-stress-disorder-ptsd/index.shtml [January 9, 2019].
3. Moss, Thorsten, and Engert, Stefan, eds. *Vom Umgang mit Schuld: Eine multidisziplinäre Annäherung* (Frankfurt: Campus Verlag, 2016).
4. Borneman, John, *Cruel Attachments: The Ritual Rehab of Child Molesters in Germany* (Chicago: Chicago University Press, 2015).
5. Buber, Martin, *Schuld und Schuldgefühle* (Heidelberg: Verlag Lambert Schneider, 1958).
6. Buber, *Schuld und Schuldgefühl*, 114.
7. Ophir, Adi, *The Order of Evils: Toward an Ontology of Moral*, transl. by Rela Mazali and Havir Carel (New York: Zone Books, 2005).
8. Card, Claudia, *The Atrocity Paradigm: A Theory of Evil* (New York: Oxford University Press, 2002).
9. Douglas, Mary, *Purity and Danger: An Analysis of Concept of Pollution and Taboo* (New York: Routledge, 1966).
10. Kant, Immanuel, *The Metaphysical Elements of Justice: Part I of the Metaphysics of Morals*, (1797), transl. John Ladd, 2nd ed., (Indianapolis, 1999), 140.
11. Duncan, Martha Grace, *Romantic Outlaws, Beloved Prisons: The Unconscious Meanings of Crime and Punishment* (New York, New York University Press, 1996).
12. Oxford English Dictionary, online, third edition, (2007), s.v. Compost.
13. Pope John Paul II, Incarnationis mysterium, §11 Bull of Indiction of the Great Jubilee of the Year 2000, (November 1998), http://www.vatican.va/jubilee_2000/docs/documents/hf_jp-ii_doc_30111998_bolla-jubilee_en.html [accessed August 16, 2016]. International Theological Commission, *Memory and Reconciliation* (December 1999), §5.1. http://www.vatican.va/roman_

curia/congregations/cfaith/cti_documents/rc_con_cfaith_doc_20000307_memory-reconc-itc_en.html [accessed July 17, 2017].

14. Pope John Paul II, Incarnationis mysterium, §11.

15. Pope Benedict XVI "The Church and the Scandal of Sexual Abuse," https://www.catholicnewsagency.com/news/full-text-of-benedict-xvi-the-church-and-the-scandal-of-sexual-abuse-59639 [April 17, 2019].

16. Ricoeur, Paul, *The Symbolism of Evil* (Boston: Beacon Press, 1968), p. 36.

17. Seligman, Adam, et al., *Ritual and Its Consequences. An Essay on the Limits of Sincerity* (New York: Oxford University Press, 2008).

18. Gibney, Mark, et. al., eds. *The Age of Apology: Facing Up to the Past* (Philadelphia: University of Pennsylvania Press, 2008). Cf. http://www.humanrightscolumbia.org/ahda/political-apologies (May 10, 2019).

19. Berger, Thomas U., *Guilt, War and World Politics after World War II* (Cambridge: Cambridge University Press, 2012).

20. Cf. the seven-part TV Mini-Series directed by White, Ryan, *The Keepers* (2017) about the Baltimore Catholic highschool Bishop McKeough (https://www.imdb.com/title/tt6792200/) or The Arte documentary *Gottes missbrauchte Dienerinnen*, first shown March 5, 2019 and then forced offline April 23, 2019. Emnonts, Benjamin, "Arte nimmt Missbrauchs-Doku aus dem Programm," *Süddeutsche Zeitung* (April 23, 2019). https://www.sueddeutsche.de/medien/arte-missbrauch-kirche-doku-1.4418540 [accessed May 12, 2019].

21. Duff, Robin Anthony, "Penance, Punishment and the Limits of Community," *Punishment and Society* (July 2003) 5:295–312.

22. Duff, Robin Anthony, "Penance, Punishment and the Limits of Community" *Punishment and Society* (July 2003) 5:295–312.

23. Peli, Pinchas, ed. *On Repentance: The Thought and Oral Discourses of Rabbi Joseph Dov Soloveitchik* (New York: Paulist Press, 1984), p. 315. Blumenthal, David R., "Repentance and Forgiveness," CrossCurrents, 48.1 (Spring, 1998); Henry Abramson, *Maimonides on Teshuvah: The Ways of Repentance,* (Touro Scholar, 2017) https://touroscholar.touro.edu/cgi/viewcontent.cgi?article=1000&context=lcas_books [January 12, 2019].

CROSSCURRENTS

# WEEDS AMONG THE WHEAT

## The Impurity of the Church Between Tolerance, Solace, and Guilt Denial

**Meinolf Schumacher**

### Pope Benedict and sexual abuse in the Catholic Church

During his visit to Germany in September 2011, then pope Benedict XVI met with victims of sexual abuse by Catholic priests and was expected to address this subject publicly. He did so only indirectly in a sermon in the Berlin Olympic Stadium, speaking in a soft voice about the "painful experience that there are good and bad fish, wheat and weeds in the Church."[1] Almost eight years later, the pope, meanwhile retired, returns to these metaphors in a comprehensive article entitled "The Church and the Scandal of Sexual Abuse":

> Jesus Himself compared the Church to a fishing net in which good and bad fish are ultimately separated by God Himself. There is also the parable of the Church as a field on which the good grain that God Himself has sown grows, but also the weeds that "an enemy" secretly sown onto it. Indeed, the weeds in God's field, the Church, are excessively visible, and the evil fish in the net also show their strength. Nevertheless, the field is still God's field and the net is God's fishing net. And at all times, there are not only the weeds and the evil fish, but also the crops of God and the good fish. To proclaim both with emphasis is not a false form of apologetics, but a necessary service to the Truth.[2]

For Benedict, the situation of the Church has evidently gotten so dire that one must be grateful to still find some good fish in the net and to spot some kernels of grain amidst all the weeds!

The disturbing element in this article is not so much what the media focused on, namely Benedict's assessment of sexual revolution in the West since the 1960s or the crisis of twentieth-century Catholic moral theology; it is doubtful that these trends contributed to sexual abuse in the Church. What is upsetting is the fact that the pope emeritus does not question the leniency of Church authorities and its exceeding forbearance, for which he himself bears responsibility, a failure that accrued grave guilt.

From a secular external vantage point, the Catholic Church appears as little more than a secret society of celibate men whose first priority consists of the protection of their members from legal prosecution of most depraved crimes and whose arcane clerical disciplines prevent any information sharing with the public. But this fails to fully explain the silence of so many bishops and priests as well as of laypersons holding church offices when questioned by state prosecutors. It is not sympathy with the perpetrators, although that complicity is less astonishing in those cases where bishops or cardinals themselves acted as sexual predators. There are other reasons, why church leaders failed to intervene energetically although they condemned and suffered the consequences of these offenses. It remains baffling why a pope who evidently feels ashamed cannot come to a consciousness of guilt, recognize and confess it, in order to make it "productive" for the victims as well as the future of the Church.[3] In the following, I will argue that it is, among others, the suggestive power of certain Biblical metaphors that restrain the response by Benedict and others.

### *Corpus Permixtum*: pure and impure in the Church

Since its beginnings, Christianity had to deal with the fact that many of its followers and functionaries did not live up to the high ethical demands, which they themselves proclaimed on the basis of the Gospels. Early on, one had to decide what should be done about "impurity" in local congregations and the Church at large, when brotherly admonitions and ecclesial penalties failed to stop minor trespasses and even serious infractions.[4] In principle, there are several possibilities: First, one can deny the existence of evil in oneself and one's group and pretend that everything is fine. This leads to duplicity and hypocrisy. The second possibility calls for violent suppression of evil in one's own ranks—which gave rise to religious terror as soon as church and state linked forces. Third, one can unswervingly exclude all impurity from the community, and thereby draw closer to the ideal of a "pure church" but only at the price of permanent reductions until one is left with a very small circle of "the pure"—who are then tempted to become self-righteous and hence impure. Fourth, one can reluctantly accept the presence of impurity and try to integrate it in some way into the Church, thereby losing the status of a pure Church. A church that claims to be pure cannot, at the same time, accept its own impurity. This disturbing idea requires metaphors that are more compelling than Augustine's idea of the *corpus permixtum*, in which he distinguished the "mixed" from the "true" body (*corpus verum*) of Christ, a confusing idea that remained relevant and effective until the Reformation.[5]

There were several Biblical stories that provided the root metaphors. One was drawn from Noah's story of the Flood in the Hebrew Bible (Gen 6:5-19), in which the church becomes the ship that traverses the storms of history. The analogy of the Church as the ark (*arca significat ecclesiam*)[6] provided allegorical-ecclesiological exegetes the opportunity to consider God's express command to Noah to save not just the clean but also the unclean animals from the Flood (Gen 7:2).[7] This unmistakably affirmed the presence of sinners as legitimate: Sinners belong in the Church and may not be excluded since God wants to save them as well. In the face of considerable resistance to this idea, the analogy was pressed further by Augustine who argued that unclean animals did not sneak onto the ark as stowaways or extort passage as pirates. Augustine writes: "Unclean animals did not break a hole according to their kind in order to secure entry into the ark. Rather, they all entered through the same door that the shipbuilder had made."[8] The inevitability of impurity, according to Augustine's *City of God*, is grounded in the notion of the Church as a world-church rather than as an elite circle of the pious: "as long as the Church is filled by many nations, it will encompass the clean and the unclean in unity until the predetermined end."[9] This also means that the Last Judgment will finish this mixture. And the Christian preachers of the Middle Ages similarly leave no doubt that this necessary mixture of pure and impure in the Church remains restricted to this time on earth. "Let us be clean animals and birds," one of them called out to his audience, "for nothing unclean or sullied will enter the heavenly fatherland" (*in coelestem tamen patriam nihil intrabit immundum aut inquinatum*).[10]

Toleration of the impure in the Church is limited to time before the Last Judgment, which breaks with the metaphorical logic of the flood allegory. There, God intends to save all of the unclean animals, so that they, like the pure animals, shall survive the Flood and increase and multiply. For this eschatological reservation, different metaphorical notions and their traditional interpretations will evidently have to come into play, namely the safe arrival of the ship of the church after its dangerous voyage across the sea of the world. In particular, there are two parables from the New Testament that were useful to address the question of the fate of the impure in the future judgment. One of these is the parable of the good and bad fish in the net:

> Again, the kingdom of heaven is like a net that was thrown into the sea and gathered fish of every kind; when it was full, men drew it ashore and sat down and sorted the good into vessels, but threw away the bad. So it will be at the close of the age. The angels will come out and separate the evil from the righteous, and throw them into the furnace of fire; there men will weep and gnash their teeth. (RSV Mt 13:47-50).

Although Matthew is above all concerned with the thought of divine judgment, which will separate the evil from the good, Christian exegesis focused on reading the dragnet as an image for a Church that includes good and bad people. Gregory the Great, who was already harking back to a long tradition beginning with Origen, preached that "we now find ourselves, good and evil, in the net of faith, like a mixed haul of fish. But on the shore will be revealed what the net of the holy Church has pulled out" (*Nunc enim bonos malosque communiter quasi permixtos pisces fidei sagena nos continet, sed litus indicat sagena sanctae ecclesiae quid trahebat*).[11]

Then, there is the parable of wheat and the tares (Mt 13:24-30), which was often linked to the story of the pure and impure animals on Noah's ark. Most recently, the church historian Arnold Angenendt used this parable for his history of religious toleration in Christianity.[12] The modern notion of tolerance, which presupposes respect for those who are tolerated, is however definitely not what these biblical passages had in mind. Tolerance is also a problematic term, when we do not merely speak of theological disagreements but rather sin and misconduct, such as corruption in the church, or simony, as well as sexual offenses, for which tolerance is principally not appropriate. Hence, we should take another look at this parable and its history of interpretation.

**"Let both grow together until the harvest"**

The parable according to Matthew reads:

> The kingdom of heaven may be compared to a man who sowed good seed in his field; but while the men were sleeping, his enemy came and sowed weeds among the wheat, and went away. So when the plants came up and bore grain, then the weeds appeared also. And the servants of the householder came and said to him, 'Sir, did you not sow good seed in your field? How then has it weeds?' He said to them, 'An enemy has done this.' The servants said to him, 'Then do you want us to go and gather them?' But he said, 'No, lest in gathering the weeds you root up the wheat along with them. Let both grow together until the harvest; and at harvest time I will tell the reapers, Gather the weeds first and bind them in bundles to be burned, but gather the wheat into my barn'. (Mt 13:24-30).

This parable is so familiar that it is easy to miss that its cogency does not originate in life experience. No farmer has ever been surprised by the fact that weeds grow amidst the grain in their field. The claim that an enemy took the effort to obtain weed seed to carefully sow it alongside recently planted good seed evokes conspiracy theories among modern readers. These are intriguing images that, above all, warn of imminent judgment and impending punishment. According to Matthew, this is the interpretation that Jesus himself provides for this parable:

> And his disciples came to him, saying, 'Explain to us the parable of the weeds of the field.' He answered: 'He who sows the good seed is the Son of man; the field is the world, and the good seed means the sons of the kingdom; the weeds are the sons of the evil one,

> and the enemy who sowed them is the devil; the harvest is the close of the age, and the reapers are angels. Just as the weeds are gathered and burned with fire, so will it be at the close of the age. The Son of man will send his angels, and they will gather out of his kingdom all causes of sin and all evildoers, and throw them into the furnace of fire; there men will weep and gnash their teeth. Then the righteous will shine like the sun in the kingdom of their Father. He who has ears let him hear'. (Mt 13:36-43).

This turns the focus entirely on the ending, the separation of good and evil, the disposal of the weeds and the punishment of the evil in the fires of hell. Nobody was more intrigued by the detail of Mt 13:30, which specifies that the weeds are bound and burnt in bundles, than Gregory the Great. To him, this signified the perfect justice of God's punishment: "Like reapers, the angels gather together the weeds in bundles for burning, whereby like is united with like in the same torment, the proud burn with the proud, the lustful with the lustful, the greedy with the greedy, the deceivers with the deceivers, the envious with the envious, the unbelieving with unbelieving."[13] The same guilt (*culpa*) receives the same punishments (*tormenta*). This provided a central trope for divine judgment day and visions of punishment in hell for medieval theology.

One often finds exhortations in the history of interpretation that ask the weed to turn into wheat, although that breaks the logic of the metaphor.[14] After all, the evil ought to receive the opportunity to change for the better. Athanasius, for example, says: "If you wish, you can change and become wheat."[15] And in a poem, Isaac of Antioch begs death to give him a postponement "until I have become a good seed of wheat."[16]

The field is most often identified as the Christian Church, although Jesus' own interpretation pointed beyond the community ("the field is the world"; Mt 13:38). The main point of the parable is almost always the command of the householder not to rip out the weeds but to let them grow till the harvest, so that they can be separated from each other at that point. Thus, Origen writes: "As the weed is permitted to grow together with the wheat in the Gospel... here too in Jerusalem...it is obviously not possible to purify the Church completely, as long as it is on earth."[17] Along with the realization that it is impossible to create a pure church, there is the warning that the damage might exceed the benefit, once the wheat is ripped out together with the weeds (Mt 13:29). John Chrysostom is thinking of violent religious war as possible consequence of attempts to rip out the weed: "And this He said to hinder wars from arising, and blood and slaughter. For it is not right to put a heretic to death, since an implacable war would be brought into the world." His second argument, as incongruous as it appears, maintains that the evil must be given the opportunity to improve and better themselves.[18] The hope that sinners "who are of unclean seed" would improve if they remained in the Church keeps showing up in sermons in the Middle Ages.

This parable served to prohibit the exclusion of sinners from the Church, or worse, their execution. It was also used to exhort good Christians not to leave the Church over the presence of impurity within the community. After all, accusations of impurity were the most important reason for schism and heresy, especially when it applied to church officials and their dispensing of the sacraments. The German word for "heretic," *Ketzer*, for instance, derives from the Greek *katharós* (clean) and refers to those who wanted to remain pure. Already Cyprian of Carthage warned critical Christians to stay in the Church: "Although there are obviously weeds in the Church, neither our faith nor our love should take offense to the point of leaving the Church, just because we notice the presence of weed."[19] Similarly, Augustine invokes this parable to argue that the assumption that one should separate oneself from the impure to prevent being tainted by their sins was nothing but arrogant impudence (*ut peccatis eorum non inquinemur*).[20]

### "Tear it out!"

Despite the clear mandate of the Gospel to permit the weeds to grow, it is quite surprising to find church dignitaries using the same image to argue the exact opposite. For instance, Pope Gregory the Great ordered the bishops of Numidia to resist all the heresies in the Church: As soon as weeds sprout amid the wheat and damages the budding harvest, the hand of the farmer must rip it up immediately with its roots, "lest the future fruit of the good seedlings are strangled by it." This is precisely where Gregory sees the task of the official Church, namely to tend the "field of the Lord" by immediately freeing the seedlings "from every weed like scandal" (*ab omni zizaniorum scandalo*).[21] Christian exegetes clearly tried to relativize the unambiguous mandate of the Gospel, which is exceptional in its protection of the weeds. More often, the thorns and thistles of vice and sins were portrayed as threatening to choke the good crop, which needed urgent and thorough purgation as primary task of those entrusted with spiritual and political affairs.

Augustine, who used this parable repeatedly in his battle against the Donatists' quest for purity, at the same time counseled Church leaders to remain vigilant: Even when one is quite certain that the good grain is firmly rooted, "the harshness of discipline should not slumber" (*non dormiat seueritas disciplinae*).[22] The position that the weed was only protected because its eradication might harm the wheat permitted merciless treatment of those identified as "weeds" in the Church. The eschatological reservation to avoid premature judgment and to await the return of the Lord (cf. 1 Cor 4:5) was readily ignored, especially once the papacy was strengthened after the investiture controversy. Now the pope acted in the seat of God. Peter Damian, for example, demanded that the pope annihilate all of the weeds that the evil enemy had sown, using the hoe of right doctrine (*sanae doctrinae sarculo*), and to separate the bad fish from the good ones.[23]

Purgation was ordinarily accomplished by earthly justice. For instance, Thomas Aquinas was forced to refute an objection to the death penalty, which had maintained on the basis of this parable that one could not remove the evil from the circle of the good by execution. That was true, Thomas conceded, but only if the good sustained damage—and the eradication of the weed threatened to rip out the good.[24] Since heresy was the worst of all crimes, Thomas was able to justify the once highly controversial execution of heretics by citing the same parable that had been used to reject it.[25] In this context, Thomas builds on Augustine's dictum that unless there was good reason to fear damage to the wheat, the severity of discipline should not be allowed to "sleep."[26] This became one important prerequisite for the Inquisition, when Pope Gregory IX ordered the Inquisitor Conrad of Marburg to begin eradicating all of the weed from the field of the Lord that the devil had sown all over Germany amid the good seed of the faith.[27] Hence, the same text, which had called for the toleration of impurity, was now deployed to justify its destruction.

### Tolerance, solace, and guilt denial

There were opponents to this merciless rhetoric in Christian literature, who spoke out in horror over the killings of heretics. In his commentary on the Psalms, Gerhoh of Reichersberg called for moderation, granting priests the authority to exercise "angelic services" (*angelica ministeria*) before the end of the world by "binding together evil vices like weeds marking them for punishment in the fires of hell, while classifying the virtuous as wheat for future heavenly reward." But, he maintained, ultimately it was not up to the priests to decide this about people "in the present-day Church." The evil remains "mixed in" until the end of the world. The Lord commands us to bear with them when he says, "let both grow together until the harvest."[28] Peter Abelard too thought that the enemy of humankind never stopped sowing weeds in the Church before the harvest, which is why schismatics and heretics had to be tolerated.[29] None of this can be called tolerance in the modern sense. Tolerance was also not the goal of humanists and reformers, quite to the contrary. Referring to the Anabaptists, Martin Luther applies Jesus' words about letting weeds and wheat grow together only to preachers, while at the same time delegating the task of killing heretics to the secular authorities, all the more energetically.[30] Zwingli and Calvin were themselves involved in gruesome executions, as we know. Disputes over the execution of heretics were likely the historical context in which the concept of tolerance was developed, arguably in the work of Castellio, who called for a kind of respect for different ways of thinking.[31] Slowly, the idea that plurality of thought does not constitute a sin against God, and therefore a crime, took root in Europe.

On the other hand, an earlier different strand of toleration existed that can be best characterized as resigned surrender to the inevitability of impurity in the Church. This is the context in which people are counseled to find solace and accept consolation for something that cannot be changed or escaped. The missionary St. Boniface, for instance, who complained bitterly to Bishop Daniel of Winchester for having to work not only with heathens, but also with sinful Christians was told about the parable of the wheat and the tares for "solace and counsel" (*solacium vel consilium*).[32] He was also reminded of Augustine's interpretation of the pure and impure animals in Noah's ark (*Et munda et immunda animalia, ut ait Augustinus, introisse in arcam leguntur*)[33] Similarly, Luther applied the parable for the consolation of the pious (*ad consolationem piorum, ne terreantur*) lest they despair over the magnitude of the infestation: "We will have to suffer it in the churches."[34] Even John Calvin offered the parable to console pastors who couldn't manage "to set the community free from every sort of filth."[35] As happens whenever solace is dispensed for situations of inevitability, this quickly morphs into justification for inaction. Augustine had already warned about this.[36] And the strict Hippolytus of Rome rebuked Callixtus I, around the year 200 A.D., for linking this parable to the ark-argument in order to get around intervening against sinners in the Church: "Moreover, the parable of the tares, he claimed, had been spoken in view of this situation. 'Let the tares grow together with the wheat'—that is, let the sinners grow in the church. Still more, he said that Noah's ark—in which there were dogs, wolves, crows, everything clean and unclean—is a symbol of the church. By this means, he claimed that it is necessary for 'clean and unclean' to be in the church."[37]

Strikingly, Pope Benedict does not endorse any of these contrasting interpretative traditions as he speaks about clerical sexual abuse today. He takes no stance on the position that either validates patience with weeds in the Church or demands their energetic uprooting. These options fade in the background as the Church suffers from a situation in which apparently nothing can be done. This may explain why members of the hierarchy like Pope Benedict show few signs of recognition of guilt. Metaphorical arguments that plead for tolerance and patience serve, by way of the idea of consolation, as justification for doing nothing or certainly not enough against violations in an institution for which one bears responsibility. It is easy to defend against guilt with reference to tolerance and excessive leniency. To change this situation in light of a "productive" guilt, this link between tolerance, solace, and guilt denial must be recognized and dissolved.

## Notes

1. https://w2.vatican.va/content/benedict-xvi/en/homilies/2011/documents/hf_ben-xvi_hom_20110922_olympiastadion-berlin.html, accessed on June 12, 2019.
2. https://www.catholicworldreport.com/2019/04/10/full-text-of-benedict-xvi-the-church-and-the-scandal-of-sexual-abuse/, accessed on June 12, 2019.
3. https://www.uni-bielefeld.de/(en)/ZiF/FG/2018Culpa/index.html, accessed on June 18, 2019.
4. Ricoeur, Paul, *The Symbolism of Evil* (Boston: Beacon Press, 1969); Schumacher, Meinolf, *Sündenschmutz und Herzensreinheit. Studien zur Metaphorik der Sünde in lateinischer und deutscher Literatur des Mittelalters* (Munich: Fink, 1996).
5. Augustine, *De doctrina christiana* III, 32, 45, ed. Joseph Martin (Turnhout: Brepols, 1962), pp. 104ff. Cf. Lamirande, Emilien, entry for "Corpus permixtum," in Cornelius Mayer (ed.), *Augustinus-Lexikon*, Vol. 2 (Basel: Schwabe, 1996–2002), columns 21–22.

6. Rahner, Hugo, *Symbole der Kirche. Die Ekklesiologie der Väter* (Salzburg: Müller, 1964), pp. 504–47.
7. Douglas, Mary, *Purity and Danger: An Analysis of Concepts of Pollution and Taboo* (London: Routledge, 1966). Blidstein, Moshe, 2015, "How Many Pigs Were There on Noah's Ark? An Exegetical Encounter on the Nature of Impurity," *Harvard Theological Review* **108**, pp. 448–70.
8. Augustine, *De fide et operibus* 27, 49, ed. Joseph Zycha (Vienna: Tempsky, 1900), p. 96.
9. Augustine, *De civitate Dei* XV, 27, eds. Bernhard Dombart, Alfons Kalb (Turnhout: Brepols, 1955), p. 497.
10. Richard of St. Victor, *Sermo* 62 in *Patrologia Latina*, vol. 177 (Paris: Migne, 1854), column 1090BC.
11. Gregory the Great, *Homiliae in Evangelia* I, 11, 4, ed. Raymond Étaix (Turnhout: Brepols, 1999), p. 76.
12. Angenendt, Arnold, *"Lasst beides wachsen bis zur Ernte." Toleranz in der Geschichte des Christentums* (Münster: Aschendorff, 2018).
13. Gregory the Great, *Dialogues* IV, 36, 14, ed. Adalbert de Vogüé (Paris: Cerf, 1980), p. 124. Also see Gregory's *Moralia in Iob* IX, 98, ed. Marc Adriaen (Turnhout: Brepols, 1979), p. 526.
14. Bainton, Roland H., "Religious Liberty and the Parable of the Tares," in Bainton, *The Collected Papers in Church History*, vol. 1 (Boston: Beacon Press, 1962), pp. 95–121; Ruggieri, Giuseppe (ed.), "La zizzania nella chiesa e nel mondo: Interpretazioni di una parabola," *Cristianesimo nella storia* **26**/1 (2005).
15. Athanasius, *Homilia de semente* 5, in *Patrologia Graeca*, vol. 28 (Paris: Migne, 1857), column 150C
16. Isaac of Antioch, *Poem about Repentance*.
17. Origen, *Homily on the Book of Joshua* 21, 1, ed. Wilhelm Adolf Baehrens (Leipzig: Hinrichs, 1921), p. 428.
18. Chrysostom, John, *Homily on the Gospel of Saint Matthew* 46, tr. Philip Schaff; http://www.ccel.org/ccel/schaff/npnf110.iii.XLVI.html, accessed on June 18, 2019.
19. Cyprian of Carthage, *Epistula* 54, 3,1, ed. G.F. Diercks (Turnhout: Brepols, 1994), p. 253.
20. Augustine, *De fide et operibus* 5,7, p. 42.
21. Gregory the Great, *Registrum epistolarum* I, 75, ed. Dag Norberg (Turnhout: Brepols, 1982), p. 83.
22. Augustine, *Contra epistulam Parmeniani* III,2,13, ed. Michael Petschenig (Vienna: Tempsky, 1908), p. 115.
23. Damiani, Petrus, *Epistula* 40, ed. Kurt Reindel (Munich: MGH 1983), p. 497.
24. Aquinas, Thomas, *Summa contra gentiles* III, 146.
25. Aquinas, Thomas, *Summa theologica* II-II. q. 11, art. 3 ("utrum haeretici sint tolerandi").
26. Aquinas, Thomas, *Summa theologica* II-II. q. 10, art, 8 ("utrum infideles compellendi sint ad fidem. In Mt. 13").
27. Cf. Kurze, Dietrich, "Anfänge der Inquisition in Deutschland," in Peter Segl (ed.), *Die Anfänge der Inquisition im Mittelalter* (Cologne: Böhlau, 1993), pp. 190–3.
28. Gerhoh of Reichersberg, *Commentarium in psalmum 64*, ed. Emil Sackur (Hannover: Hahn, 1897), p. 486, 489.
29. Abaelardus, Petrus, *Theologia christiana* IV, 72, ed. Eligius M. Buytaert (Turnhout: Brepols, 1969), p. 298.

30. Luther, Martin, "Ob christliche Fürsten schuldig sind, der Widerteuffer unchristlichen Sect mit leiblicher straffe, und mit dem schwert zu wehren" (1536), *Werke*, vol. 50 (Weimar: Böhlau, 1914), p. 13.
31. Castellio, Sebastian, De haereticis, an sint persequendi (1554); https://www.e-rara.ch/bau_1/doi/10.3931/e-rara-32986, accessed on June 18, 2019.
32. Boniface, *Briefe*, ed. Reinhold Rau (Darmstadt: WBG. 1968), p. 188 (Letter 63).
33. Boniface, *Briefe*, p. 198 (Letter 64).
34. Luther, Martin, "Annotationes in aliquot capita Matthaei" (1538) in *Werke*, vol. 38 (Weimar: Böhlau, 1912), pp. 558–9.
35. Calvin, John, "Commentarius in Harmoniam Evangelicam", in *Opera*, vol. 45 (Brunswick: Schwetschke, 1891), column 369.
36. Augustinus, *De fide et operibus* 27, 49, p. 95.
37. Hippolytus of Rome, *Refutation of All Heresies* IX, 12, 22-23, tr. M. David Litwa (Atlanta: SBL Press, 2016), pp. 655–7.

# PURITY AND KASHRUT

**Deborah Williger**

The dialectic of impurity is expressed by the old German proverb *Dreck macht Speck*, meaning "filth makes bacon." This sounds like a non-kosher introduction to the topic at hand, but the proverb articulates that children, like piglets, will put on weight once they ingest a certain amount of filth from their environment. This absorption increases the variety of intestinal germ population, which has been demonstrated to promote robust growth. On the other hand, there is the saying *Vor dem Essen, Händewaschen nicht vergessen*, warning "don't forget to wash your hands before you eat." This claims the opposite: Certain impurities cause dangerous illnesses. Therefore, it is necessary to cleanse dirt that could be harmful and pose a risk to health and life. Infiltration by impurities must be prevented before they do damage. Both physical and psychological contaminations can affect individuals or groups. Spiritual contaminations that dominate one's entire existence fall, following traditional Jewish interpretations, into the category of idolatry. Worshiping foreign gods is a capital crime. The transgression of the commandment against making images, represented in the Hebrew Bible as the dance around the golden calf, is considered unthinkable.

Measuring degrees of spiritual pollution seems impossible. By contrast, the natural sciences have no problem quantifying the exact doses and potential costs and benefits of pollution in a variety of environments. Once a critical mass of impurity enters a living organism, it can do harm. If the infected organic mass cannot be healed, it dies. The creatures' organic mass disintegrates into its molecular units, and its bare skeletal remains emerge clean and purified. In the end, death makes a clean separation between organic and inorganic matter, while life presupposes the commingling of both unconditionally. Living organisms are characterized by diversity and movement. Organic and inorganic elements exchange, mix, mingle, and separate in rhythmic cycles. There is constant metabolic exchange between chemical elements, such as nitrogen, oxygen, and carbon; mineral building blocks, such as phosphorus, calcium, or iron; and various organic components, such as carbohydrates, enzymes, hormones, and amino acids in tissues, vessels, organs, and cellular nuclei. Living organisms, whether single or composite cell organisms, constantly establish a fluid equilibrium between internal and external elements. Life flourishes where separation and recombination, division, and fertilization occur. Once certain parts no longer come together in order to multiply, distances widen and borders emerge that eventually lead to permanent divisions, and life ends.

It seems high time to develop new methods for cleansing and healing. Despite considerable scientific progress in the development of tools and technologies, all the way to computers and artificial intelligence, humanity has not succeeded in creating a more just and happier world. We continue to inflict poisonous ideologies, such as antisemitism, racism, and exploitation on each other, despite our technological progress and intellectual prowess. Furthermore, the evolution of human civilization has created unintended side effects, including population growth and mass production and consumption, as well as increasing levels of pollution that threaten the planet. The greatest threats emanate from the smallest particles, especially the waste products of nuclear fission. Radioactive and other forms of environmental pollution are postmodern forms of original sin that implicates all descendants in the future who did not commit the original offense. As this enormous mass of guilt piles up, what are the possibilities for expiation and atonement? Will there even be a possibility for reconciliation so that life will continue on earth? We do know that neither systemic nor individual violence can be purified by tears. That requires action. There is no point in waiting passively for redemption, as if a redeemer (a man) could arrive to undo the consequences of environmental pollution. The Jewish tradition is focused on right action. According to the Torah, one should never expect metaphysical interventions or the entry of divine forces into earthly affairs.

Purification is a means of defense. For spiritual or physical hygiene, the following cleansing agents are available: reconciliation, teshuvah, time, water, sand, salt, and the medical arts. These different detergents have varying degrees of efficiency. In vain, Lady Macbeth tried to wash her hands to regain innocence. The success of purification depends on the manner and form of the pollution, as well as the adequacy of the detergent and its appropriate application. Whether we speak of the purification of objects or subjects, and irrespective of the choice of methods, purification is always a process of separation.

In fact, creation itself is the result of a process of separation. Out of one totality emerged many parts. Kabbalists call this origin of the world *zimzum*, and astrophysicists name it the Big Bang. From duality flowed immeasurable evolutionary diversity without ever-reaching perfection. According to the Kabbalists, the two primordial rivers that flow from the Garden of Eden (Gen 2:10-14) signify the fusion of wisdom and cognition.[1] While logic separates, abstracts, and analyzes, wisdom connects and clarifies. In the first act of creation, God says "Let there be light" (Gen 1:3), which allowed perception of the created universe, heaven, and earth. Enlightenment makes the infinite potential and its interconnectedness, the dependence, and interflowing of all reality recognizable.

Following in the footsteps of ancient Greek philosophy, the notion that the physical body is of lesser worth than the rational mind (historically correlated with masculinity) became powerfully entrenched in the socio-history of the West. The source of impurity was identified as the material world, while the spiritual was seen as pure. This alienation between body and spirit paved the way for dualistic systems of domination, including social Darwinism, sexism, and the domination of animals, which I define as jugularism, from the Latin word *jugulare,* meaning to slaughter or murder.[2]

In Jewish thought, spirit and body are not antagonists. Instead, physical health and intellectual-spiritual health form a unity. Maimonides (1135–1204), a physician and rabbi, prescribed dietetic treatments, which required the maintenance of balance in all domains of life as the best prophylactic for general good health as well as righteous action following the commandments of God.[3] The capacity for good and evil is inherent in all people, who must decide every day to choose the right path. In the first book of Moses, there is a constant search for peace by way of balance. The social dynamics between the first pair of brothers, Cain and Abel, all the way to Joseph and his brothers is the story of transformation of male violence into moral strength and balanced relationships. It is through just action that humanity becomes connected to fellow creatures, an ideal vision described in the Garden of Eden, which serves as blueprint for the Messianic world to come.

Jewish dietary laws, *kashrut*, orient the just preparation and presentation of food in the direction of the metaphysical. Jews are bound together by their trust in the truth of the Torah and its Talmudic interpretation. They observe these commandments voluntarily, out of insight, in humility and gratitude. *Kashrut* is one of the pillars of the Torah, Talmud, and Jewish teachings. It serves to maintain purity and balance of body and soul. *Kashrut* devotes itself in almost infinite detail to practical instructions for the proper preparation of food and defines prerequisites and modes of contamination. The rules of *kashrut* connect to various commandments and prohibitions that serve a range of different goals, from just food preparation to the proper celebration of the yearly cycle of religious holidays, from the sustainable use of natural resources to practices of hospitality and charity. *Kashrut* is embedded in the entire Jewish system of morality and law, *Halakah. Halakah*, "the way," consists of 613 commandments, of which 248 are positive commandments and 365 are negative prohibitions. Some of these commandments relate to the Temple service and have lost their relevance with the destruction of the Temple some 2,000 years ago. All others remain in effect without distinction. In general, *Halakah* orders conduct on the basis of two principles: to avoid suffering and to maintain proper balance.[4] Jews are instructed to behave justly, every day, for their entire lifetime. There is no need for rational justifications. Rational explanations are not considered necessary or theologically desirable, although they are sometimes requested and provided. But anyone who follows the revealed commandments unconditionally walks with God.

Transgressions of God's ordinances constitute a sin against God. But humans are imperfect and everyone makes mistakes. Accepting one own sinfulness is the beginning of purification, growth, and maturity. Everybody is summoned to insight, expiation, and atonement, and nobody should be abandoned in the process of purification of their guilt. On Yom Kippur, a fast day of atonement, the entire congregation confesses every conceivable sin and asks for mercy for all of them together. Anyone who repents and commits to change may hope for reconciliation and longevity. The rabbis of the Talmud and Jews today are constantly debating the legal, practical, social, and moral issues in search of compromise and the right path. There is agreement that no position can ever claim to be the sole and unique truth.

The rules of *kashrut* guide proper behavior toward living animals in general, and the process of preparing food from animals in particular. The welfare of animals plays a central role and supersedes human use. The Talmud claims: "If animals suffer, it can never go well for humans" (jBaba Mezia 85a). Therefore, numerous Jewish directives and prohibitions demand considerate care for animals. Humans are explicitly prohibited to torture animals and charged with the ethical treatment of animals. Animals have a right to live in species diverse environments, based on Genesis: "Be fruitful and multiply in all kinds" (Gen 1:25). All species including humanity are part of divine creation. There is no living being that is intrinsically clean or unclean. There can be no hierarchy or value judgment among fellow creatures. The issue of clean and unclean arises exclusively in the context of suitability for temple sacrifices, and nowadays, with regard to status as a source of nourishment. Impureness counts as *treyf*, which is Yiddish and refers to foods deemed unfit for human consumption on the basis of *kashrut*. Eating *treyf* food pollutes body, mind, and soul. Hence, the rules of *kashrut* aim to prevent human pollution by controlling the process from selection to consumption. An animal must be chosen and declared pure for later consumption, it must be slaughtered, cut up, sliced, prepared, and brought to table as a meat dish, and at every point of this process, something could go wrong and render it *treyf*, in which case it must be passed up and sorted out of the process of further preparation. I divide this process into four stages: The first step is the choice of pure animal species from all animal species. The second step deals with the application of *kashrut* rules for the slaughter of the (sacrificial) victim chosen from a pure species. The third step involves the choice of body parts of the slain animal that qualify as pure for further preparation. The fourth step regulates the separation of meat and milk, which must be kept separate at all phases of preparation and consumption of the meal. At each of the four steps, there are feedback mechanisms that control the process and determine the next step until the final determination that a meal qualifies as kosher for consumption.

Different Jewish movements apply different *halakic* standards to kashrut practices in their communities. For communal meals in congregations, large kitchens, restaurants, or private homes, a rabbinically trained *mashgiach* or *mashgicha* (male or female kashrut supervisors) controls the observance of dietary laws. Congregational rabbis teach their congregants and give the seal of approval on packaged food to certify their kosher status, the *hecksher*, the guarantee that every step was correctly observed throughout the production process. This precedent is being adopted by modern secular practices that mark merchandise for quality (organic) and provenance (origin country), which becomes more popular.

There are numerous criteria for selection at each stage. I can only provide a quick overview here. First, the question of which animal is considered clean and from the right animal pool that is permitted for slaughter. Leviticus specifies all of the clean and unclean water, air, and land animals. Already in the book of Genesis, Noah distinguishes between pure and impure animals, which seems anachronistic since the flood occurs before Sinai. Of the pure animals, Noah takes seven pairs with him on the *teva*, the ark. Without this precaution, his thanksgiving sacrifice after the *mabbul*, the Great Flood, would have exterminated the pure species immediately.

The majority of kashrut rules concern land animals and poultry, and specifically herd animals that can be domesticated, bred, and kept in close proximity to human habitation. Their controlled reproduction in captivity under good conditions guarantees a sustainable herd size that provides a continuous supply of animals for transportation and fieldwork, as well as wool, milk, eggs, and meat as well as hides and horns to livestock owners.[5] But on meat consumption, the Torah places restraints protecting domestic animals from unrestrained use, mandating that they should be treated as if they were free and wild animals that could be caught only with difficulty (Dt 12:20-22). *Kashrut* aims to protect the life of animals by limiting the desires of humans and moderating the consumption of meat. Such boundaries serve as purifying discipline to generate moral maturity. There is no commandment in the Bible that demands any consumption of meat. On the contrary, the ideal form of nourishment is veganism, as laid out in the account of creation (Gen 1:29). Toward this ideal, *Halakah* helps imperfect humans to tread the path of moderation.

No predatory animal belongs among the clean species. Nachmanides (1194-1270) remarked that the prohibition to eat predators existed to prevent the transfer of the bloody manner with which predators feed themselves to humans.[6] His explanation provides a moral reason for the ban on eating predators. Spiritual health and purity, he seems to argue, is at risk of becoming bloodthirsty and must be protected by dietary laws. There is only a low threshold that prevents humans from turning violent and brutal, according to the Talmud, and it must be fortified by various measures. For instance, this subject comes up in the context of training ritual slaughterers and is cited as reason for the requirement to cover up the spilled blood of slaughtered animals immediately. One is allowed neither to collect nor to use blood. The possibility of psychological pollution from gazing on large pools of blood is taken very seriously. In the Book of Job, blood should even be covered with gold dust, should there be no other material available (Job 28:6). Meat should only be eaten by righteous people, who are morally mature to resist acts of violence: Without inner strength and purity, one risks losing gentleness by consuming meat.

Pigs are likewise spared. One explanation for this is that the Israelites wanted to separate politically and culturally from the Canaanites and Egyptians, who ate pork. In addition, pigs cannot graze on pastures and compete with humans for food. In barren steppe regions, pigs were kept at latrines, a circumstance that associated pigs with uncleanness. Agrarian science tells us that in hot climates, pork is prone to contamination by bladder worms and various germs that spoil their meat more quickly than the flesh of ruminants. That might have been recognized phenomenologically 3,000 years ago and provides a reason for abstinence from pork. Today, pigs are pumped full of soy meal and grain for mass consumption, which could calm fears of hygienic pollution. As to the moral and spiritual pollution possibly caused by the mass consumption of pork, that is a different matter. After all, behavioral science attributes high intelligence and sensitivity to pigs, which can reach the level of six-year-old children. Pigs are physiologically closer to humans than primates; their skin, bones, organs, and muscles are similar to ours. I suspect there might be a sensibility against cannibalism at work here. On the other hand, all of the prohibitions are subordinated to the principle of saving a life (*pikuach nefesh*). For example, there is a Talmudic discussion about whether a pregnant woman could decide to eat pork on Yom

Kippur.[7] Purity laws are strict but always directed toward enhancing life and greater abundance.

Why was the Jewish abstention from pork taken as a provocation throughout history, often leading to violence against Jews? In earlier centuries, Christians persecuted Jews with crude depictions of so-called *Judensäue*, meaning Jewish sows. In Spain, Jews who saved themselves from burning at the stake of the Inquisition by submitting to forced baptism were called *maranos,* meaning pigs. Jewish purity laws were turned against Jews by Christians who defamed Jews as spiritually inferior and dirty like animals.

Donkeys, as valuable beasts of burden, were not eaten. One possible explanation is that donkeys give birth to only a few young and they were very rare and needed to be conserved. Camel meat was likewise not consumed, probably because of the sheer impossibility of slaughtering large animals gently. And considerate slaughter is a necessary condition.

Ritual slaughter also specifies the qualities of the particular animal that is chosen for slaughter by a professionally competent examination of its fitness. Any externally visible or palpable physical defect or impairment, such as old or open injuries, would disqualify an animal from slaughter. An injured animal could not be slaughtered. That disqualifies hunting. The hunt does not allow for careful exclusion of animals with flaws or their suffering in the process of killing itself. The mandate for physical integrity of animals before slaughter and the commandment to respect the life and fertility of the animals also exclude castration. Eunuchs were excluded from serving as Temple priests. Temple priests were not allowed to come into contact with the dead, which renders them impure temporarily.

Purity laws, of course, extend beyond food and slaughter regulations. People can also become ritually impure but only for certain periods of time, and there are means of purification. Time is one factor in purification. A person who shows signs of leprosy remains impure until the wounds heal up. Time heals wounds. Healing is a form of purification, and purification promotes healing. The concept of quarantine reflects the French word for forty, *quarante*. Forty days of rain, the Great Flood, a quarantine against the violence of the epoch. Forty is the biblical time unit signifying completion, a generation (in the desert), that is needed for purification and maturation. In the barren wilderness of sand, the souls of the Israelites could be purified without going astray. The regeneration of the soul and of nature requires periods of rest, *Shabbat*. Noah, whose name in Hebrew means "resting," spent 365 days on the ark surviving the purifying wrath of the flood. Water and sand are enough to cleanse dishes, materials, and bodies. But oceans and deserts are necessary to purify souls. The judge Deborah ruled for forty years of unity and peace in Israel. Forty years of wandering in the desert were needed in order to appreciate the freedom following the exodus. What can cleanse our world today, since water, soil, and time are in short supply?

Ritual purity and impurity fluctuate in and through time. For instance, menstrual ritual purity laws regulate sexual relations through the menstrual cycle and after childbirth. Women's menstrual blood and the bloody discharge of childbirth do not render women dirty but ritually impure. Impurity in this context carries no moral implications, since menstruation is a natural and ordinary part of the rhythms of life. A patriarchal gaze that objectifies women and reduces them into property of their husbands sees the monthly *mikveh* bath as a ritual preparation that readies women "for use." But there are other possible interpretations that appreciate menstrual purity laws as regular periodization of sexuality in order to recharge eroticism in the context of marriage. The period of purity and impurity mandates phases of rest, regeneration, and purification. Traditionally, women have been in charge of *Niddah* laws and they invested their performance with personal and spiritual meaning, including the pleasurable preparation for sexual encounter.

*Shabbat,* as well, establishes a living rhythm that structures holy and profane by introducing distinctions between feast day and workdays. As a day of rest, the *Shabbat* is sanctified by observance. The *Shabbat* is consecrated as a day of collection and peaceful assembly. In the creation narrative, the *Shabbat* is not closed off like the days before it with the formula, "and it was evening and it was morning." On the sixth day, all living creatures receive provisions, and there is a double portion of *manna* for the Israelites on their journey through the desert. Material well-being is secured before the *Shabbat* begins. Of all the days, God makes the seventh day of creation holy, dedicated to God self. The *Shabbat* points beyond itself and Jews receive an additional soul on that day. It is a day to regenerate so as to face the coming week until the next *Shabbat.*

Pure animals are not holy animals. Animals chosen as sacrifice in the Temple were dedicated to God. But if an animal, after consecration, injured itself on the way to the altar or proved inappropriate for any other reason, there was a firmly established withdrawal procedure. Kashrut does not sanctify the flesh. There is no Catholic mystery of transubstantiation taking place here. Holy animals never wandered through Jerusalem. While *kashrut* facilitates no esoteric metamorphosis, it serves to sacralize Jewish life.

The rules for ritual slaughter are found in the book *Kodashim* (sacred things) of the Talmud, in the tractate *Hullin*, which addresses ordinary or mundane matters. This section, in translation, comprises about 900 pages. These are the written records of the oral Torah that relate to the verse in Deuteronomy: "Thou shalt slaughter from your livestock as I have bidden you" (Dt 22:21). No question is left unanswered as the sages discuss who should do the slaughtering and when, where, and under which conditions an animal may be killed. Its level of detail can be compared to today's European Union slaughterhouse quality management manuals. According to the laws of kashrut, an animal has to be killed gently and its blood has to be drained completely. A well-trained *Shochet* slaughters an animal in one sharp deep cut, which slices through all of its neck parts toward specific chondral of the spine. Animals show no pain reaction to these cuts and are brain dead within seconds.[8] A thorough inspection of the carcass, the *bedika,* follows. If everything has gone according to order, and the carcass shows no damages, body parts considered non-kosher, such as entrails, brain, and nerves, must be separated. There was never any risk of BSE (bovine spongiform encephalopathy), which causes mad cow disease and created a major food and veterinarian crisis in Europe between the 1980s through the early 2000s. The next step involves processing sections of meat in a kosher kitchen. Before cooking, meat must be further koshered with water and salt, that is, completely cleaned of blood. Most importantly, meat is kept strictly separate from dairy during storage, preparation, and serving. The separation of milk and meat goes back to the Torah verse: "Thou shalt not boil a young goat in its mother's milk" (Ex 23:19). Three more injunctions warn against taking a mother bird out of its nest with its chicks (Dt 22:6-7), specify that "a calf and its mother must not be slaughtered on the same day" (Lev 22:28), and warn against wanton destructiveness (Dt 20:19).

Maimonides drew from these verses that humans should practice compassion and moderation and avoid greed that harms creation.[9] Hence, the separation of dairy and meat is endowed with moral meaning and spiritual lessons. My explanation points to the barren landscape of Israelite pastoral communities who for reasons of herd management had to adjust their consumption of meat and milk to herd size and grazing conditions. Resources (albumen) can be spared if the luxury of consuming meat and milk together is moderated. There is a wait time that must be observed between consuming dairy products and eating meat. Dairy and meat cooking utensils and dishes must be separated and, as practical aid, are often color-coded, so that blue hand towels are used for dairy and red for meat. Dishes have to be koshered, which today is entrusted to dishwashers that clean with hotter water than hand washing ever could. Although several assortments of dishes are no longer necessary, traditional households maintain separate sets of meat and dairy dishes.

Modern research has shown that storing fresh meat and milk products in separate freeze units decreases the likelihood of bacterial cross-contamination. Separate storage units for unprocessed foods and processed meat and milk products are mandated by European and national jurisdictions and strictly regulated by governmental nutrition, hygiene, and veterinary institutions. All (even non-kosher) supermarkets and butcher shops separate their food items. Other research tested the rise of carcinogenic nitrosamines when meat and dairy products are heated together. Thus, *kashrut*, with its ancient millennia-old traditions, displays features that turn out to be relevant for health and ecological reasons. In the 1970s, Rabbi Zalman Schachter Shalomi founded the Renewal movement and used *kashrut* for holistic and ecological purposes. Ecological crop and animal husbandry, which aim at sustainability, animal welfare, and fair-trade practices, make up today's image of *eco-kashrut. Eco-kashrut* is a growing ecological movement in the United States and Israel. It is even attracting followers in Europe, such as the Renewal community Ohel Hachidusch in Berlin.

But in Europe, there is very little knowledge about kosher food. Its infrastructure has been almost completely destroyed in the Shoah, and the Jewish remnant cannot sustain a robust demand for kosher products. There is nothing that comes close to what existed in Europe 90 or 100 years ago. Ironically, it was frenzied ideas of racial purity that spawned this murder, a fatal utopia that contrasts with traditional Jewish notions of ancestry and elective affinity (2 Kings 2:12). German guilt contaminates and creates an obscure bond between Germans and the Jewish people. There is a peculiar attraction to Jewish cuisine and culture despite the alienation and estrangement from Jewish people. In absentia, Jewish food enjoys a good reputation and seems compatible with people's understanding of healthy nourishment. Maybe, food will succeed in creating rapprochement as the proverb says: "Love goes through the gut."

Even as opposition to global unification grows, there is a hunger for different, genuine, and original cuisines. Against the trend of national isolation, people engage in a vital blending when it comes to food. Getting to know foreign cuisines promotes mutual respect for what is different. There is a surge of interest in dishes and cuisine coming from the furthest ends of the earth. Ayurveda, *eco-kashrut,* and Japanese tea ceremonies fascinate for their holistic approaches to nutrition. It is not only empirical material qualities but their moral, spiritual, and sociopolitical aspects, including the protection of animals and the environment that make them attractive. This trend toward exotic, authentic regional dishes rules extends to kosher cuisine as well.[10] In the United States, kosher restaurants and food stores are gaining new customers. Consumers eat kosher pastrami one day and traditional Thai food the next. They trust the qualitative tests of a rabbinate whose authority they would not respect otherwise. Dairy kosher cuisine is vegetarian and must be prepared without any trace of animal meat products. Meat is supplemented by exclusively vegan food with vegetable albumin and fat. That makes certain lines of kosher products attractive as vegan and vegetarian alternatives.

On the side of the traditionalists, there is a tendency to circle the wagons. It never occurs to many traditional Jews, for example, that something essential is missing from their Jewish identity, when they turn their back on the needs of animals, nature, and the environment. They should face the world around them and include ecological themes in kosher rules. It would be much more productive if both traditional and critically minded types would realize that their basic goals are in agreement: to maintain species biodiversity, as well as cultural and religious variety, on the earth.[11] Variety and mixture (impurity) strengthens and enriches life. That can already be seen in the microcosm of intestinal bacteria populations.

Purity and impurity are ambivalent constructs that can be harmful and beneficial. Total purity means death, while life requires exchange, variety, and mixture. All living organisms are characterized by impurity in their genetic makeup, bloodlines, families, cultures, and species. The purity rules of kashrut aim for connection with the divine, with nature, with others, humans, and with oneself. The *kosher* kitchen serves life, contributes to sustainable management of natural resources, and embraces the search for vegan and vegetarian alternatives.

## Notes

1. Green, Arthur, *A Guide to the Zohar* (Stanford: Stanford University Press, 2004), pp. 40–4.
2. Williger, Deborah, 2019, "Jenseits der Grenzen," *Journal of the European Society of Women in Theological Research* 27, pp. 109–32.
3. Rabinowitz, Louis I., and Philip Grossman, ed. and transl. *The Code of Maimonides: The Book of Holiness*, 5, (New Haven: Yale University Press, 1965).
4. Does a future of high-quality farmed meat on the basis of tissue culture lead to more or less meat consumption? While it makes animal farming obsolete, it does not change the dualistic and "jugularist" perspective on animals, which requires a more profound paradigm change.
5. Berkowitz, Beth, and Marion Katz, "The Cowering Calf and the Thirsty Dog," *Islamic and Jewish Reasoning*, Anver M. Emon ed., 69–112 (London: Oneworld, 2016).
6. Nachmanides, *Commentary on the Torah: Deuteronomy*, Chavel, Charles B. ed. (New York, Judaica Publisher, 2005), p. 271.
7. Mosche ben Maimon, *Von verbotenen Speisen*, Igor Itkin/Alexander Adler/Leon Mandelstamm (www.talmud.de/tlmd/rambam-von-den-verbotenen-speisen) chapter 10.
8. Ritual slaughter (kashrut and halal) aims to slaughter with care and compassion. In the United States, a mobile pen for ritual slaughter was invented by animal science professor Temple Grandin. The animal is led into the pen and secured in a fixed position by hydraulic lifts, which keep the dead animal from falling. The carcass is cut only after all of the blood has drained, according to rules of Halakha. This process has been tested on over 3,000 slaughtered cows and certified by the **A**merican **S**ociety for the **P**revention of **C**ruelty to **A**nimals. It is known as A.S.P.C.A.-PEN and used by small-scale organic farms in the United States. Grandin, Temple, *Improving Religious Slaughter Practices in the US* (Fort Collins, TX: Anthropology of Food, 2006).
9. Marder, Michael, *Maimonides' Palm Tree*, in The Philosophers Plant - An Intellectual Herbarium (Columbia: Columbia University Press, 2014), pp. 97–110.
10. Schorsch, Jonathan, *The Food Movement, Culture, and Religion – A Tale of Pigs, Christians, Jews, and Politics* (Palgrave Macmillan Cham, 2018), pp. 29–34.
11. Cardozo, David, "The Symbolism of the Korban Pesach," *Cardozian Newsletter*- Nissan 5779, https://www.cardozoacademy.org/?s=Nissan.

# "CLEAN" COLLECTIONS

## On the Idea of Contamination in the Provenance Discussion

**Roger Fayet**

Debates over provenance and how to handle museum objects are increasingly using the vocabulary of "clean" and "unclean" to characterize objects that are thought to be in some way "contaminated" by their histories.[1] This essay will first give some examples for this discussion and then examine theoretical assumption behind the notion of contamination that transfers certain problematic events linked to guilt into the essence of objects. Beyond that, I am interested in knowing whether this makes any sense and should be continued.

The terminology of "clean/unclean," "contaminated," and "toxic," as far as I can tell, first arose noticeably in the context of the Gurlitt case.[2] When Cornelius Gurlitt donated his art collection to the Bern Museum of Art, some were referred to as "clean" paintings—meaning unproblematic and admissible to the art collection of the Museum, while others were considered "contaminated" and even "toxic." When the media reported about the contract signed between the Bern Museum of Art, the Federal Republic of Germany, and the Bavarian State Ministry for Justice on November 24, 2014, they emphasized that only the "clean works" of the Gurlitt collection were to be admitted into the Museum. For instance, the *Berner Zeitung* writes on June 29, 2017: "Since 2014 the complete body of work, which contains many works of classical modernism, has been carefully examined. According to the contract of the Museum of Art with the German authorities, only 'clean' paintings are to be permitted to come to Bern."[3] This means concretely that any work suspected of being looted was not to be handed over to the Museum but was to remain in Germany in order to be returned to its rightful owners. In their statements, those responsible for the Museum used the same terminology. Marcel Brülhart, vice president of the board of trustees of the Bern Museum of Art, told the *Schweizerische Depeschenagentur* in November 2016 that the Museum would not accept works that "are not clean in their provenance."[4] A year later, the Swiss tabloid *Der Blick* quoted Museum director Nina Zimmer saying that all of the works shown in the Gurlitt exhibit are "clean," and none are under suspicion for being looted art. Asked by the *Berner Zeitung* about the state of provenance investigation in the Bern Museum of Art in general, then director Matthias Frehner replied that the Museum has "a clean inventory practice."[5]

In another vein, the notion of "clean" paintings also appears, when writers insist that cleanness can never be restored. Thus, the art critic Philipp Meier commented on the contents of the exhibit in the Bern Museum of Art for the *Neue Zürcher Zeitung*: "All of them are 'clean' works, and hence under no suspicion for being looted art [...] But has this art been, as it were, washed clean? Of course not. It remains part of their history. And this filter will always cloud the view of them."[6] As early as February 2016, Philipp Meier, together with Luzi Bernet, conducted an interview with the President of the World Jewish Congress, Ronald Lauder, who declared with references to the acquisition practice of art collector Emil Bührle: "Good faith doesn't make these paintings clean."[7] The interviewers liked this remark so much that they turned it into the title for the entire interview. About the Bern Museum's taking over the Gurlitt collection, Lauder said: "What's the good of that? The whole Gurlitt collection is contaminated."[8] The art critic Hans-Joachim Müller even suggested in *Die Welt* on this context that such "stains" adhere to the paintings: "One cannot—and that above all is the lesson from the meritorious self-examination of the Bern Museum—simply wipe away the history of these paintings with research. It will always stick to them—like stains that cannot be removed with anything."[9]

With the word "contamination" from the Latin *contaminare*, to soil or defile (German *besudeln*), yet another term from the semantic field of the pure and impure makes its appearance in the discussion of provenance. As mentioned, Lauder uses the adjective "contaminated" to characterize the Gurlitt collection. An article published in the *Neue Zürcher Zeitung* in

2017 by domestic news editor Jörg Krummenacher about paintings in the St. Gallen Museum of Art and their fate during the Nazi period bears the title "Contaminated Paintings." He criticized the lack of information about the provenance of the paintings and asked: "Are they or aren't they contaminated by their history in Nazi Germany? With one exception the Museum of Art makes no mention of this."[10]

The adjective "toxic" ratchets up the metaphor of contamination another notch, implying a threat to life. In November 2017, the *TAZ, die Tageszeitung* published a commentary by art editor Brigitte Werneburg about the various roles played by the Bern Museum of Art and the Federal Republic of Germany, which she calls, with some irony, "ingenious" as a path of least resistance. Switzerland, she says, gets to avoid "toxic paintings" while focusing on the "cheerful" side of the issue, while Germany gets to feel satisfaction for successfully coming to terms with its past. "The toxic paintings, which remain under the cloud of suspicion for having been stolen from Jewish collectors during the Nazi period are exhibited in Bonn, where Minister of Culture Monika Grütters patted herself on the back at the opening [of the critical exhibition of the Gurlitt collection in the Bundeskunsthalle Bonn]."[11] Cultural journalist Thomas E. Schmidt similarly declared in his mostly objective article titled, "Guilt and Atonement," first published in *Weltkunst* and then *Zeit Online*, that the Gurlitt collection will have to be "examined by the task force to distinguish between harmless and toxic parts, starting in February, 2014."[12]

### On the meaning of objects

Where does the notion come from, that certain historical events could somehow render an object "unclean," "contaminated," "stained" or leave some mark, which renders this object dangerous? We know the phenomena from everyday experience, as well as from various cultural contexts, that particular objects, such as memorabilia, carry more and different meaning and value than their functional use, aesthetic value, or originally intended signification. The current owner derives a sense of connection, by means of the object, to another person, such as the previous owner. By association, this implies that something of the character of the previous owner (strength, wisdom, authority) carries on and is transferred to the person who owns the object now. The object is seen as representative of specific events, or particular ideas and values. What a thing means

—to those for whom it is *meaningful*—can have very little in common with what a disinterested observer sees in it.

In the loft of my parents' house, there were two trunks, one of wickerwork and the other of wood (possibly a hope chest), with imitation woodwork and the initials of the original owner inscribed on it. My father, who had inherited the trunks, had a sharply defined emotional-normative attitude toward these two objects. He dearly loved the wickerwork trunk because he received it from an aunt, who along with her husband had fought as volunteers in the Spanish Civil War on the Republican side and carried their belongings back to Switzerland in it. The wooden trunk, however, he saw as a symbol of the harshness and greed of his grandmother, who owned several rental properties and demanded the surrender of objects of values from her tenants every time they could not pay their rent on time. I have maintained the semantic charge of these two trunks, following my parents, and they express similar meaning to me. However, with the passage of time, in my view they have fused together and represent different aspects of my family history; they have taken on a more narrative than normative perspective.

There are many elaborate cultural and sacral practices that charge objects with meaning, such as the construction and veneration of memorials, which are not necessarily statues and buildings created just for this purpose, but sometimes consist of ordinary objects or regular places, which have been touched by certain events (such as the death of a famous public figure). Relics are another eminent example for this type of semanticized objects, which include not only the physical remains of saints, but their garments and other objects (such as cloth that was briefly placed on their corpse). Such objects could be sold and show the pervasive assumption of "contagious" transferability of certain qualities and effects.

Museum objects are another category of things charged with meaning. In fact, being loaded with meaning constitutes the precondition for admission into a museum. Objects are collected, stored, and exhibited, because they are seen as representative signs for certain historical, social, artistic, or natural phenomena. Their signifying power and permanence comprise their peculiar strengths in the context of the transmission of knowledge, and their material participation in what they represent gives them the power to testify, at least to some extent. The ethnologist Karl-

Heinz Kohl argues that objects in museums are the modern equivalent of sacred objects, with which they share essential qualities, such as the loss of their practical functions, their symbolic nature, their separation from the everyday world, and their removal from the economic cycle[13]—even if they do not possess revelatory power and do not serve the most important function of sacred objects, namely as epiphanies. But sacral objects as well as museum objects show that it is possible to load things with certain meaning that is not intrinsic to the objects themselves. Many cultural practices build upon this feature of the object. As Kohl argues, "on the basis of their concreteness and solidity, objects lend themselves especially well to the embodiment of memories, ideas, and feelings, which can be transported across time and space and thereby assume some permanence. In this respect, they seem superior even to language, which is a much more fleeting and unstable medium."[14]

## The concept of semanticization

There has been much reflection and publication on the signifying function of museum objects. Since the 1970s, semiological museum theory has examined the relationship between things and meaning built on the analogy between language and the medium of exhibitions. For instance, in an 1972 essay, American museum expert and then director of the Brooklyn Museum Duncan F. Cameron compared exhibitions to a semilinguistic system, in which objects are arranged in such a way, complemented by textual and design elements, that statements develop that are comparable to sentence structures: "the language of the museum depends on the object as noun, the relationships between objects as verbs, the groupings or displays of objects as cohesive statements (patterns rather than sentences or paragraphs), and in all of this the supplementary media of print, graphic, photograph, film, and the line, colour and form of object environment are the adjectives and adverbs."[15] For the museum expert Ivo Maroević, the referential function of objects is the peculiar feature of museum objects. Upon entry into the museum, they are no longer merely identical to themselves but function as signs for a reality, which transcends them: "Museality is the quality of objects of the human cultural heritage by which they function in a specific reality as documents of another reality."[16] Krzysztof Pomian has coined the proficient term "semiophore" (i.e., sign-bearer) to refer to those objects that are candidates for museification or (in the days before museums existed) were chosen for collection. The term "semiophore" implies their dual nature, its lower level or material carrier and its upper level that signifies meaning. In principle, loading matter with meaning does not depend on any particular kind of matter or specific social locality. The trunks in my parents' attic can serve as semiophores. But for objects to make their way into a museum collection, "they must turn into semiophores, whatever their original status may have been."[17] I myself have proposed to complicate this understanding of a thing as a simple or unified sign, by a theory of objects as conglomerates of several signs, that is, as plural signs.[18] This, I believe, is of considerable importance to understand the problem of the multiple meanings of objects.

The multiplicity of meaning is a feature of objects, which makes them problematic, notwithstanding Karl-Heinz Kohl's celebration of the medial use of things as superior to language because of their concreteness and permanence. In this context, Maroević even speaks about multiple identities of a museum object and concludes: "The identities of the museum object allow for a broad spectrum of possible interpretations of the object's world in the museum communication."[19] There is no medium, argues Cameron, that seems to be harder to work with than the museum exhibition.[20]

But there is a crucial difference between the notion that objects are loaded with extrinsic meanings and the idea of contamination: In the first case, the relationship between material object and meaning is somewhat arbitrary and entirely situated in the mind of viewer (another viewer can "read" the same object differently, which is permitted under this premise), while the concept of contamination presupposes a change in the material substance of the object. Of course, there are some semiotic approaches with similar tendencies to materialize meaning in the object by way of certain images and metaphors. For instance, Michael Parmentier, eminent German scholar of education who died in 2018, formulated the relationship between object and meaning suggestively as "things acquire different meanings in the course of time that—to put it somewhat roughly—remain attached to them, and cling to them in successive layers like the rings in a tree trunk, so to speak."[21] Similarly, Felwine Sarr and Bénédicte Savoy argue in their report on the restitution of cultural objects expropriated by colonialists, *Restituer le patrimoine africain*, that the meanings ascribed to an object in different places leave a sort of physical deposit that becomes part of its essence.

> Once they have been displaced, the objects endure a variety of processes and experiences of successive re-semanticization, and have undergone an excessive imposition of several layers of signification. [. . .] How are we able then to restitute to these objects the sense and functions that once belonged to them, without neglecting the fact that they had been captured and then reshaped by a plurality of semantic, symbolic, and epistemological dispositives for more than a century?[22]

It is certainly correct to observe that people who view and handle certain objects perceive changes in meaning and identity. But from an epistemological perspective, we must insist on the difference between changes in the semanticization of objects and the idea of a contamination that would change their very essence. While semiotic theories of the object such as those of Pomian, Maroević, or Cameron start from the assumption of the plasticity of the construction of meaning, which includes and extends to all things, the concept of contamination asserts the possibility of irreversible pollution of things that come into contact with problematic events. Furthermore, mere contact with the source of pollution is assumed to have the power of alteration. The idea of contamination is based on notions of *spheres* of contamination in which anything that comes into contact within widening circles of polluting events, persons, or ideas risks infection and defilement by association.

It makes a big difference whether we base our reflections of museum objects that have been involved in histories of violence, injustice, and guilt on either the theory of semantic meaning or on notions of the contamination of things. If we act on the logic of contamination, objects with a history of violence must be considered substantially altered in dangerous ways that pose a threat to their present-day environment. It becomes imperative to remove such objects as quickly as possible or at least to keep them at a safe distance, in order to safeguard museums as places of purity and value. There is no alternative, since the essence of these objects has been affected by contamination. If, on the other hand, we consider objects merely charged semantically with meaning, a charge that remains open and subject to change, then their history becomes a matter of the *interpretation* of these events, with different semantic meanings possible and to be determined in each *particular* case. Objects are not defined by a common moment of contamination, but their perception occurs within a diversified and pluralized field of interpretations, that is potentially complex, contradictory, and complementary. Interpretations are continuously modified and replaced by new meanings, as the context of perception shifts, and the function, content, or history is interpreted differently. On that view, it is not only possible to store and exhibit items with problematic provenance in museums, but museums would be ideal places to mediate such problematic histories while keeping the possibilities of new, alternative, and different interpretations open.

### The Emil Bührle collection

The idea of contamination is particularly relevant in the debate over guilt-laden artworks in the collection of Emil Bührle, which will be put on display in the Zurich Museum of Art.[23] The industrialist Emil Bührle, who came from Pforzheim and lived in Zurich since 1924, amassed an important collection of art during the years from 1936 to 1956 including masterpieces of French Impressionism and Post-Impressionism, which he supplemented with notable paintings by the Old Masters and medieval sculptures. After his death in 1956, one third of his collection was placed in a foundation set up by his descendants, which became accessible to the public in a private museum starting in 1960. It was located in a residential building right next to the Bührle Villa, where he had stored parts of his collection. In 2015, this museum was closed for reasons of security and the collection is scheduled to move to its permanent home in 2022, once the expanded wing of the Zurich Museum of Art is completed.

The Emil Bührle collection aroused particular attention, not just because of the quality of the works it contains—among others, Courbet, Manet, Degas, Renoir, Monet, van Gogh, Gauguin, Picasso, and Braque—but also because of the circumstances surrounding their acquisition. Before he was called up for military service in 1914, Bührle had studied, among other subjects, art history in Freiburg im Breisgau and Munich. He began building his art collection in 1936. First, he limited himself to the Swiss art market. In 1939, he participated in an auction of the Gallery Fischer, which sold paintings confiscated from German museums as "degenerate art" by the Nazis. He had no success, but beginning in 1942 he succeeded in acquiring more and more works by the French Impressionists from the Gallery Fischer. He made more purchases from, among others, the art dealer Fritz Nathan, who had emigrated from Munich to St. Gallen in 1936, and helped other emigrants sell their artworks to museums and private collectors. Around 100 of the 633 works that Bührle ultimately acquired came into his possession during this time. In contrast to the collector Oskar Reinhart from Winterthur, Bührle was not particularly scrupulous about provenance.[24] By the end of the war, it turned out that thirteen art pieces had been looted in occupied France. After a trial at the Swiss Federal Court's chamber for looted art, Bührle had to return these works to their proper owners. But a few years later, he repurchased nine of the paintings for a second time. After 1948, Bührle employed a secretary and curator who was responsible, among other things, to research into the origins of the paintings. Today, the provenance of all the works has been documented and is available for viewing on the Internet, including those parts of the collection that are not owned by the foundation but by the Bührle heirs.

The troubled reputation of the Bührle collection derives not only from the uncertain circumstances of some of his acquisitions but from his professional activities, in which he showed as little scruples as in building up his collection. He began his career in 1919 in his father-in-law's tool manufacturing factory in Magdeburg. In 1923, the firm bought the Swiss Machine Tool Factory in Oerlikon, which Bührle took over as director in 1924 and which he acquired in 1937 as the sole proprietor. The manufacture of arms and war material became the main business of the Oerlikon Bührle & Co. Machine Tool Factory, which over the decades delivered its products to China, Japan, Germany, France, Great Britain, North and South America, Turkey, and the Soviet Union, among others. Until 1940, France and Great Britain were important costumers, but after the occupation of France when Switzerland was completely surrounded by Axis powers, he began to sell exclusively to the latter. Before the war was over, the firm was put on the blacklist of the Western Allies, but with the beginning of the Cold War, the Western powers started buying military weaponry, including anti-aircraft systems, from Bührle's factory again. The sale of military material by Oerlikon Bührle & Co. became the subject of a detailed investigation by the Independent Expert

Commission of Switzerland—Second World War. In 2002, the Commission concluded, among other things, that the delivery of armaments to the German Reich and Italy was carried out with the support of the Swiss government and that the weapons deliveries, which consisted mainly of anti-aircraft missiles, were not of relevant military significance.[25]

### Contamination or semanticization

The Bührle collection is such an instructive example because we are not dealing here with a case that concerns restitution of certain objects in a collection, or a lack of research into provenance, or a lack of historical knowledge about the person of the collector. There are few collections for which the provenances of the works have been so thoroughly researched. Looted art was restituted, early on by order of a court. Some of these works were acquired a second time, after Bührle made restitution for their theft. His activity as a collector as well as his professional activity as director and owner of a military weapons factory that sold armaments before, during, and after the Second World War have been academically investigated, and the moral implications have been thoroughly discussed. What remains, however, is the fact that the collection contains works of art with a history of Nazi theft—and the rest of his collection is in the company of the further. Moreover, we have a situation where the collector acquired a major portion of his fortune through the production and sale of weapons. If we view the collection today under the premises of the logic of contamination, their elements are "unclean" because they were either directly implicated in actions that were unjust or at least ethically dubious, or they have been contaminated although they themselves are neither legally nor ethically problematic simply by association or contagion as part of the entire complex of the collection. On that view, the museum must distance itself unless it wants to contaminate itself by integrating the collection, thereby becoming guilty for benefitting from guilt-laden objects. By contrast, if we proceed on the semantic theory of "charged" meaning of works of art, the museum creates the public forum in which the history of Bührle's collection can be debated permanently. In that case, the ethical ambiguities of certain historical events also come to the fore, as for instance the fact that acquisitions from refugees, when paid fairly, may have contributed to help people raise funds who were in desperate need for cash.

In the discussion over the admission of the Bührle collection into the Zurich Museum of Art, the logic of contamination marks, for instance, the position of member of the Zurich City Parliament, Markus Knauss, who argued that the collection Bührle was "contaminated in many ways."[26] Similarly, historian Thomas Buomberger and art historian Guido Magnaguagno in their publication *Schwarzbuch Bührle: Raubkunst für das Kunsthaus Zurich?* (The Bührle Black Book: Looted Art for the Zurich Museum of Art?) speak explicitly of "contaminated paintings"[27] and "incriminated blood-money paintings."[28] They conclude that the integration of the collection should only be considered advantageous "if not a single work retains any shadowy traces."[29] They also consider the possibility of "a public-political initiative to completely refuse admission of the Bührle foundation's collection on permanent loan and to instead stock the new rooms with the work of the many and outstanding anti-fascist artists from Zurich."[30] These calls for outright rejection of the collection are contrasted by the initiative of the city and canton of Zurich to commission a research project to contextualize the person of Emil Bührle and his collection, submitted by the Research Center for Economic and Social History of the University of Zurich.[31] The results of this research will be used in the exhibition of the collection. This can be considered as a scholarly form of semanticization of a collection's art objects.

The concept of semanticization is far better equipped to take into account the multiplicity of meanings of objects than essentialist arguments about contamination. It highlights the reality of the variability of meaning. It is also indicative of a culturally productive interaction with guilt. Without escaping into non-committal relativism—since the variability of semanticization is not the equivalent of arbitrariness—it allows for communication about the past, while maintaining the possibility of dissent. It does not aim to conceal historical injustice and moral failure, but rather encourages its acceptance. At the same time, it does not reduce the object to a certain segment of its history, but respects the presence of older—as well as more recent—histories. The question of guilt or of the morality of agency is not defused but rather becomes the point of negotiation among participants in the debate—it materializes and becomes "thinged," as Bruno Latour once explained in a pun referring to the relationship of "thing" in the usual sense of the word to "thing" as the term for the governing assembly of early Germanic communities.[32]

## Notes

1. The author thanks his colleague Peter Schneemann, University of Berne, for drawing his attention to this phenomenon.
2. This refers to the discovery and confiscation of the collection of Cornelius Gurlitt in 2012, which he had inherited from his father, the art dealer Hildebrand Gurlitt. The collection in Munich comprised about 1280 works, mostly of the classical modern period; later discoveries in a domicile in Salzburg increased the collection to over 1,500 works. About a third of the works was suspected to be Nazi-looted art. So far, however, this has only been confirmed in a few cases. After the death of Cornelius Gurlitt in 2014, it became known that he had designated the Bern Museum of Art as his sole heir. The museum has taken over those works that are under no suspicion of looted art.
3. Feller, Michael, and Florine Schönmann, "Schwierigkeiten bei der Ausfuhr der Gurlitt-Bilder," *Berner Zeitung*, June 29, 2017, https://www.bernerzeitung.ch/region/bern/schwierigkeiten-bei-der-ausfuhr-der-gurlittbilder/story/23792756, accessed on June 17, 2019.
4. sda, Schweizerische Depeschenagentur, "'Wir bereuen es nicht, das Gurlitt-Erbe angenommen zu haben,' Marcel Brülhart, Vizepräsident der Dachstiftung des Kunstmuseums Bern, äussert sich zum Rechtsstreit um das Gurlitt-Erbe," *Der Bund*, September 18, 2016, https://www.derbund.ch/bern/kanton/wir-bereuen-es-nicht-das-gurlitterbe-angenommen-zu-haben/story/20780681, accessed on June 17, 2019.
5. Cf. Maurer, Christian, "Endlich am Licht, was Gurlitt verbarg," *Der Blick*, November 2, 2017, https://www.blick.ch/life/heute-oeffnet-im-kunstmuseum-bern-die-wichtigste-ausstellung-des-jahres-endlich-am-licht-was-gurlitt-verbarg-id7543, accessed on March 10, 2019.
6. Meier, Philipp, "Gurlitt-Kunst in Bern: Die 'Kunst-Opfer' treten in den Zeugenstand," *Neue Zürcher Zeitung*, November 2, 2017, https://www.nzz.ch/feuilleton/wiedergutmachung-an-der-kunst-ld.1325655, accessed on June 17, 2019.
7. Bernet, Luzi, and Philipp Meier, "'Guter Glaube macht Bilder nicht sauber,' Interview mit Ronald S. Lauder," *Neue Zürcher Zeitung*, February 3, 2016, https://www.nzz.ch/zuerich/guter-glaube-macht-bilder-nicht-sauber-1.18688461, accessed on June 17, 2019.
8. Ibid.
9. Müller, Hans-Joachim, "Diese Kunstbeute der Nazis gibt weiter Rätsel auf," *Die Welt*, April 26, 2016, https://www.welt.de/kultur/kunst-und-architektur/article154772103/Diese-Kunstbeute-der-Nazis-gibt-weiter-Raetsel-auf.html, accessed on June 17, 2019.
10. Krummenacher, Jörg, "Kontaminierte Bilder," *Neue Zürcher Zeitung*, February 16, 2017, https://www.nzz.ch/schweiz/stgallens-zeigt-kunstwerke-aus-der-nazi-zeit-vergiftete-und-entgiftete-bilder-ld.145917, accessed on June 17, 2019.
11. Werneburg, Brigitte, "Kommentar Gurlitt-Ausstellung: Geniale Rollenverteilung," *TAZ, die Tageszeitung*, November 3, 2017, http://www.taz.de/!5457569/, accessed on June 17, 2019.
12. Schmidt, Thomas E., "Sammlung Gurlitt: Schuld und Sühne," *Zeit online*, September 30, 2017, https://www.zeit.de/kultur/kunst/2017-09/cornelius-gurlitt-umgang-raubkunst, accessed on June 17, 2019.
13. Cf. Kohl, Karl-Heinz, *Die Macht der Dinge: Geschichte und Theorie sakraler Objekte*, Munich: C. H. Beck, 2003, p. 154.
14. Ibid., pp. 120–21.

15. Cameron, Duncan F., "Problems in the language of museum interpretation," *The museum in the service of man: today and tomorrow. The museum's educational and cultural role. The papers from the Ninth General Conference of ICOM*, Paris: ICOM International Council of Museums, 1972, p. 91.
16. Maroević, Ivo, "Die Museumsausstellung als museologische Herausforderung," *Museum aktuell* 83, 2002, p. 3521.
17. Pomian, Krzysztof, *Des saintes reliques à l'art moderne: Venise – Chicago, XIII*[e] *– XX*[e] *siècle*, Paris: Gallimard, 2003, p. 157.
18. Cf. Fayet, Roger, *Die Logik des Museums: Beiträge zur Museologie*, Baden (Switzerland): Hier und Jetzt, 2015, pp. 29–48.
19. Maroević (2002), p. 3522.
20. Cf. Cameron (1972), p. 90.
21. Parmentier, Michael, "Die Dinge und ihre Zeichen: Ein etwas polemisch geratenes Plädoyer für eine strukturale Analyse musealer Gegenstände," *Mitteilungen & Materialien, Zeitschrift für Museum und Bildung* 49 (1998), p. 35.
22. Sarr, Felwine, and Bénédicte Savoy, *The Restitution of African Cultural Heritage: Toward a New Relational Heritage*, trans. Drew S. Burk, Paris: Ministère de la Culture / CNRS / ENS Paris Saclay / Université Paris Nanterre, 2018, p. 30.
23. With regard to transparency, the author points out that in his function as Associate Professor at the University of Zurich he is a member of the board of trustees of the Bührle Collection.
24. Cf. Francini, Esther Tisa, et al., *Fluchtgut – Raubgut: Der Transfer von Kulturgütern in und über die Schweiz 1933–1945 und die Frage der Restitution* (Veröffentlichungen der Unabhängigen Expertenkommission Schweiz – Zweiter Weltkrieg, 1), Zurich: Chronos, 2001, pp. 108, 414, and 454.
25. Cf. Hug, Peter, *Schweizer Rüstungsindustrie und Kriegsmaterialhandel zur Zeit des Nationalsozialismus: Unternehmensstrategien – Marktentwicklung – politische Überwachung* (Veröffentlichungen der Unabhängigen Expertenkommission Schweiz – Zweiter Weltkrieg, 11), Zurich: Chronos, 2002, pp. 795, 802–5, and 809.
26. Stadt Zürich, Gemeinderat, *Auszug aus dem substanziellen Protokoll, 121. Ratssitzung vom 26. Oktober 2016*, item 2369, https://www.gemeinderat-zuerich.ch/Geschaefte/detailansicht-geschaeft/Dokument/22ca59a1-b733-411c-b477-1d8a33083028/2016_0409%20Protokollauszug%20substanziell.pdf, accessed on June 17, 2019.
27. Magnaguagno, Guido, "Die Sammlung Bührle: Raubkunst und Fluchtgut," in Thomas Buomberger, and Guido Magnaguagno, *Schwarzbuch Bührle: Raubkunst für das Kunsthaus Zürich?*, Zurich: Rotpunktverlag, 2015, p. 118.
28. Ibid., p. 127.
29. Buomberger, Thomas, and Guido Magnaguagno, *Schwarzbuch Bührle: Raubkunst für das Kunsthaus Zürich?*, Zurich: Rotpunktverlag, 2015, p. 9.
30. Ibid., "Vorbemerkung zur E-Book-Ausgabe, Dezember 2015" (preliminary remarks on the E-Book issue, December 2015).
31. Cf. https://www.fsw.uzh.ch/de/personenaz/lehrstuhlleimgruber/Forschung.html, accessed on June 17, 2019.

32. The pun originates from an unpublished lecture by Bruno Latour, held as part of the conference *Im Reich der Dinge: Das Museum als Erkenntnisinstrument,* Deutsches Hygiene-Museum in cooperation with Max-Planck-Institut für Wissenschaftsgeschichte Berlin, Dresden, May 6 to 8, 2004.

# SHIT BUCKET CAMPAIGNS AND NESTBESCHMUTZER

## The Waldheim Affair in Austria

**Iris Hermann**

On June 8, 1986, in the second round of elections, Kurt Waldheim was elected President of Austria. Up to that point, he could look back on a great diplomatic career: For ten years, he had held the important office of General Secretary of the United Nations and he had previously served as Foreign Minister of Austria. But after his election, nothing in Austria remained the same. His election, his person, and his conduct caused a political firestorm that changed the foundations of the Republic of Austria. The point was less the public exposure of a Nazi perpetrator than how the nation chose to remember Nazi crimes, and the kinds of obligations and responsibilities that arose from these crimes for individuals.

Waldheim was not accused of being a war criminal. Even the World Jewish Congress, which performed a thorough investigation and would not have hesitated to charge him, did not accuse him of specific crimes; he was never indicted or convicted of concrete wrongdoing. What aroused animosity was the way in which he "doctored" his career, hid his actual whereabouts during the last years of the war, and lied about his proximity to the executed war criminal General Löhr in Yugoslavia. He must have had knowledge of mass murders, even if he did not personally participate. Instead, he claimed lapses in memory, denied his membership in the Storm Troopers, and spun ever more fantastic tales, which failed to explain anything. Doron Rabinovici, a writer, historian, and member of the Republican Club, which was founded during the Waldheim Affair as the public voice of the opposition, said this about Kurt

Waldheim: "How he had dealt with his past between 1945 until then was pathetic and unacceptable. He embodied everything we fought against. Waldheim's lies were important not because they were personal character flaws, but because they revealed the broader political strategy. We knew our Waldheimers. They relied on antisemitism as a dog whistle. Fiery yellow placards went up all over Vienna announcing in blazing red script: 'We Austrians will elect the man ***we*** want'. Such slogans targeted Jews, although it was by no means only Jewish officials who wondered how it was possible that an intelligence officer serving in the Saloniki region could claim ignorance about the deportations leaving Greece."[1]

I have chosen this affair for this essay on "impurity and guilt" because both sides, Waldheim opponents and Waldheim supporters, confronted each in the semantic field of filth (German: *Dreck,* which is closely associated with "shit") deploying this terminology in ever more creative ways to attack opponents. I will use two examples from different media: first, Robert Schindel's grand Viennese novel, *Der Kalte,* which is often read as an account of the Waldheim Affair.[2] There is the figure of Johann Wais, who shares many features with Waldheim. And there is an abundance of references to filth, particularly in their Viennese manifestation. More on that later.

The second example is the Austrian documentary film, *Waldheim's Waltz*, by Ruth Beckermann, which was shown at the Berlin Film Festival and nominated as the Austrian entry for the Oscar.[3] It contains many original recordings from Waldheim's electoral campaign, the charges of the World Jewish Congress, as well as footage from the political campaign launched by Waldheim opponents, whose numbers kept growing and whose arguments gained traction.

First, I will use these examples to show how denunciation, accusation, criticism, and defense make use of the semantic field of filth and thereby construct an entire lattice of meaning that will be analyzed here. In a second step, the concept of guilt will be unfolded within this frame of reference. Guilt is here a particularly complex phenomenon, since Waldheim was never legally charged with a criminal offense but incurred guilt in the moral realm that required significant explanation and effort at description. Methodologically, it must be pointed out that my sources are fictional works of art rather than primary sources. The primary source material has been thoroughly examined by linguist Ruth Wodak who deserves credit for analyzing the media reports about the Waldheim affair in various print formats. Her work shows that it was Waldheim himself who first used the terminology of dirt. For instance, the *Neues Volksblatt,* the official newspaper of the conservative Austrian People's Party (ÖVP), which supported Waldheim's nomination, reported on March 24, 1986:

> The repulsive witch hunt against independent presidential candidate Kurt Waldheim is getting dirtier and dirtier. First his political opponents Blecha and Ischer have charged him with "Memberships during the Nazi Period" on the basis of archival records, and now the Jewish World Congress has struck over the weekend with the news that Waldheim was wanted as a suspect for "participation in murder." Waldheim responded: "a new high point in the dirt campaign."[4]

"Dirt campaign," "shit bucket campaign," or sometimes just abbreviated as "the campaign" expressed clearly what Waldheim thought of the criticism he received for his inexplicable memory lapses, which excluded significant segments of his life, particularly the years before 1945. To him, this was merely an attack on his integrity, an unjustified blow below the belt aimed at harming him politically and obstructing his election. The novel *Der Kalte* takes up this interpretation and discusses its implications for the figure of Johann Wais:

> How could one smear this UN-VIP so that the muck spurts? Now I will have to suffer through the beautified life memories, presumably prepared by his press officer Novacek. In America, a dozen people would have performed background checks. But here, people believe every folk tale that is dished out.[5]

The fictional speaker of this text is an employee of the SPÖ chancellor, who deliberately seeks to find dirt in order to smear the candidate Waldheim, but in reality it was neither the Social Democratic Party nor the Communist Party that accused Waldheim. They remained passive throughout this affair and were not its instigators, as Viennese journalist Georg Tidl, who examined the history of the Waldheim affair, has concluded.[6] In the novel, *Der Kalte*, it is the alter ego of Simon Wiesenthal, by the name of David Lebensart, who blames the Social Democrats for exaggerating the gaps in the biography of Waldheim, saying: "The Social Democrats are fishing for filth everywhere."[7] Later, there are references to Dr. Wais' obsessive concerns with "soiling," while trying to maintain his "pure conscience" and his sense of humor.[8] Robert Schindel rewrites the history of the Waldheim Affairs. While Waldheim remained in office for the full six years of his presidential appointment, the figure of Johann Wais resigns and concedes to the demands of the opposition.

### Cleansings

While political opponents are often smeared in political campaigns, Waldheim was a particularly fitting target. He had spent his previous life as a high-ranking intelligence officer in the Wehrmacht in very close proximity to "cleansing campaigns." In the novel, Schindel attributes the following internal monologue to Waldheim, which I will quote at length:

> I still do not understand why this campaign is heating up despite my frequent explanations. Now they are pestering me about the battles in the Koraza region [in Bosnia-Herzegovina]. Of course, I cannot remember everything all of the time. Foolishly, I claimed that I had never been there. Now Novacek discovered that, indeed, I was there when the cleansings began. So what? I was not involved, or else I would have remembered. I was always happy that I did not participate in interrogations, although I reported their results. Well, sometimes I had to be present, especially with the Susiĉ people, a most dangerous gang of partisans. Of course, we did not use delicate methods, after all it was war, and the cruelty of partisans was legendary. One had to be merciless, fighting them. I viewed them as enemies back then, because that is what they were, and we were *their* enemies, basta. Good Lord, I have never been a weakling, but I never participated in retaliation killings. Others volunteered and enjoyed it, even some of my good friends, who are not facing any charges. My General Löhr, however, paid for it with his life, they decapitated him—or maybe they shot him. Why am I thinking about this? Johann Wais turned around, went to his desk, and looked at the telephone. Captain Plume was responsible for the deportation of prisoners during the Kozara operation. I had to help him, he was my superior, but I only signed the

> papers. I never even looked into the faces of any of these individuals—or did I? And even if I looked at some of them? They were immediately sent off to Semlin [at the outskirts of Belgrade] to be housed there as prisoners of war. Some of the partisans were obviously civilians, that is always the case for partisan fighters, hence the accusation that we killed civilians... people are clueless, but keep spitting at me.[9]

There are not many metaphors of cleanness/uncleanness in this fictional stream of consciousness, but they appear at crucial moments: For instance, Wais [whose name resonates with weiss, meaning "white") uses the term "cleansings," which refer more accurately to "ethnic cleansings." They are considered war crimes, and Wais would be considered a war criminals, if he admitted his participation. But Wais avoids this, as he articulates his surprise over the continuation of the attacks despite his soothing explanations. The president elect of the Republic of Austria is no longer invited by Western governments, and the United States has put him on a watch list. The author uses venomous words, which are intensely physical, such as the word "angeifern," which evokes images of attack dogs straining against their leashes, their spittle spraying from aggressive barking. Wais feels "spat at."

Schindel's novel uses the Waldheim Affair and interweaves it with several other postwar stories, for instance, the story of Edmund Fraul, a camp survivor and veteran of the Spanish Civil War who fought on the side of the International Brigades and is still a tireless champion of the cause of justice. But trauma has extinguished his emotions, which he rarely expresses in his personal life, if he feels their presence at all. In the novel, Edmund Fraul is about seventy years of age and experiences another turning point in his life. He begins a conversation with Wilhelm Rosinger, who was a guard in Auschwitz and responsible for the murder of at least seven children in the concentration camp. He was punished after the war, served time in prison, and has since been released. Strangely bound together as victim and perpetrator, in what sociologists have called "negative symbiosis," Fraul insists that they share stories about Auschwitz. As they recount stories and swap experiences, it becomes clear that they have Auschwitz in common. A catharsis is happening, which releases both: Rosinger feels deep repentance and confesses his guilt to Fraul. Fraul mourns for the dead Rosinger and experiences long-buried feelings rise to the surface in long spasms of weeping. The novel oversimplifies this catharsis, which happens too quickly, is too conciliatory, and lacks depth. But it is noteworthy that this segment of the novel makes no references to impurity or purification. There is no reference to washing away any guilt, as the semantic field of uncleanness is absent. The theme reappears in a different section of the novel, where a survivor of the Shoah describes her side of the "cleansings," which plunged her life into filth and darkness. This woman from Bukovina recounts:

> "I was fourteen years old when the Nazis invaded the Soviet Union, and my home town of Czernowitz [now western Ukraine] came under the control of the Romanian fascists. We lived in Kobilanska Street; my parents ran a press that put out books about art. I went to the gymnasium [high school]. As Jews, we were forced to move to a ghetto and later deported to Transnistria. I am the only member of my family who survived. There was nothing there except filth and starving people, corpses, diseases, stench—Transnistria, that was hell."[10]

### The Nestbeschmutzer and the dung heap

The term *Nestbeschmutzer* was pervasive and used as a blanket term to refer to any opponent of Waldheim as a way to insult and defame them, by Waldheim as well as by others. It became so commonplace that critics reclaimed the term and used it as a battle cry to unify the opposition. For instance, the previously mentioned "Republican Club," which became active in the political struggle, published a book called "The Art of Nest-fouling."[11] Schindel's novel *Der Kalte* retells the scandal that attended the opening performance of Thomas Bernhard's theater play "Heldenplatz" in Vienna in 1988. Heldenplatz is the name of the square in front of the Hofburg Palace, where Hitler announced the *Anschluss* [annexation] of Austria to Germany before an enormous crowd on March 15, 1938. The well-known writer Thomas Bernhard was commissioned by the politically controversial German theater director Claus Peymann to write a theater play to mark the one-hundred-year anniversary of the Austrian National Theater in Vienna, the Burgtheater in 1988. The play was kept strictly secret before its first performance. But a journalist had been tipped off and published some excerpts from the theater text, which caused public outrage. The Austrian public resented the impending "defamation of Austria" and the "nest-fouling" that would be performed on stage in Bernhard's "manure piece" [*Sudelstück*]. In protest, on the day of the premier, a truck of manure was unloaded in front of the main entrance of the Burgtheater on Heldenplatz. As Schindel retells the scene in his novel:

> Around four p.m. a large truck appeared before the Burgtheater. It parked illegally before the entrance of the theater. Two men in overalls climbed out of the cab, walked to the back of the truck, opened the cargo area, jumped up and began to use pitchforks to dump piles of manure, straw drenched with cow urine and dung. A policeman began to approach the scene, eyed the two men. The driver, a strong, fat fellow with a shaved head, stood in front of the hood and gazed calmly at the cop, who stopped, scratched his neck, and retreated. People began to gather around the growing dung heap and expressed their appreciation and sympathy. One person shouted "Cover the Burgtheater in shit." Some people laughed, and more people gathered. Finally, both men climbed down from the truck, each lifted a bucket from the cargo area and dumped its contents on the dung heap. The viewers standing closest to the pile pulled back. Before the men drove away—the license plate was smeared with filth and hence illegible—they threw leaflets into the crowd, with the printed message "THROW THE BASTARD SCHÖNN OUT OF AUSTRIA."[12]

The figure of theater director Peymann is renamed Schönn in Schindel's novel, but otherwise it follows the historical events closely. The words of Johann Wais come true in reverse fashion: The critical theater performance is covered in shit, as the metaphorical shit bucket hit the venerable Burgtheater. Of course, this attempt to disturb or block the premiere of the theater play failed spectacularly, as Thomas Bernhard's play *Heldenplatz* only gained publicity and notoriety.

### The Waldheim Waltz

Ruth Beckerman uses original footage from Waldheim's candidacy in Vienna for her documentary film that was released in 2018. She was also an original member of The Republican Club around Doron Rabinovici, and she had been opposed to Waldheim's presidency and been active in the struggle to change Austria's culture of denial and forgetfulness. Beckermann dramatically assembles visual material that in many respects complements Schindler's fictional account of the Waldheim Affair. Most striking is a scene toward the end of the film, in which Waldheim prepares to deliver his first speech as President of the Republic of Austria. He is waiting to go live before the cameras, which are already rolling: The makeup artist wipes and powders his face several times, a garishly uniformed cleaning lady vacuums and cleans all of the surfaces around him, an assistant brushes fluff off his dark suit. These silent cleanup operations speak volumes. Waldheim is preoccupied, the film suggests, with the correct fit of his suit and the perfect facial mask that will hide his flaws and failings as he faces the nation. The film captures a cultural moment of intense battles over moral impurity and the overwhelming desire for cleanliness, correctness, and blamelessness.

**Clean hands, white vests, and skeletons in the closet**

In the field of Austrian literature, the Waldheim affair served as pivot that dislodged the Austrian legend as the first victim of Nazi Germany, which was first voiced by the Allied victors. Austria, however, was not invaded and subjugated by hostile German forces. Austrians followed Hitler into war gladly and volunteered in droves for service in the SS. Waldheim was a member of the SA and had done much more than his mere duty as a "decent" soldier. When he began to lie about his biography and cover up his actual career path during the war years, groups of activists demanded more truth and accountability in Austrian politics. There was some disagreement over the precise role of Waldheim in this cultural transformation. Some, like Robert Menasses, claimed that Waldheim was a mere speck in the morass of Austrian politics: "Every Austrian," he said, "believes that Austria is a double victim, first at the hands of the National Socialists, and then again at the hands of the anti-fascists. But in reality, Austria is only the victim of Austrian fascism, of the Dollfuss regime [Engelbert Dollfuss, conservative Austrian Federal Chancellor, 1932-1934, who was assassinated] and its disciples and descendants. That is the only real situation of victimization in Austria. Waldheim, by contrast, is something like the dirt under my fingernail, if we measure him against the real problems of Austria."[13] Others, like Schindel and

Rabinovici, give more credit to the culture shock unleashed by the Waldheim Affair, which jolted a younger generation into critical confrontation with Austrian history. I agree that the Waldheim affair produced more than a little irritating dirt stuck under one's fingernail and compelled a shift toward greater nuance in guilt discussions that took note of the "real" victims of National Socialism. These victims suffered not only at the hands of major perpetrators and the regime's mass murderers but also because mere "bystanders" and complicit enablers failed to intervene. Now, everybody wanted to forget what they had done. Waldheim became the paradigm for the desperate and pathetic desire to forget. Even if he did not actively kill another human being, he was certainly morally complicit as an officer in a regime that committed atrocities. This debate over responsibility, accountability, and guilt became unstoppable after Waldheim, no matter how strong the threats of libel and denunciation, the smear campaigns, and manure piles were.

It is important to note the moment in which metaphors of filth are invoked, and when they remain irrelevant and impotent. As soon as guilt has been confessed, when regret has been expressed and forgiveness requested or granted, guilt no longer appears as impurity; there is no need to wash it off, and one cannot befoul or tarnish such as person (Viennese: "*anpatzen*"). The imaginary of filth is virulent only as long as guilt remains hidden and denied. Metaphors of filth signal the presence of remainders that refuse to vanish and that cannot be forced to disappear. While it has traditionally been the political left that was tarnished as filthy and dirty, in the postwar debate over the moral and political legacy of National Socialism, both camps used the imagery of filth in creative and concrete ways. In the case of the manure pile on *Heldenplatz,* Austria's largest newspaper, the *Kronen Zeitung,* spoke of self-sullying to indicate that those who dared to ask critical questions about the "brown" Nazi past were the cause of pollution. For the newspaper, the problem originated with the Nestbeschmutzer and those who presumed to criticize Austria. Still, the actions of a few courageous activists succeeded in changing the culture of remembrance in Austria, which required confronting sometimes painful memories.

Recently, the sudden appearance of the so-called Strache-videos, which exposed shady dealings between an extreme right-wing Austrian politician and a Russian oligarch, the semantic field of filth, swung back into operation in full force. The public release of these secret videos recorded in a villa in Ibiza was called part of a dirt campaign, and they forced the resignation of Austrian vice president Heinz-Christian Strache, followed by the collapse of Chancellor Sebastian Kurz's entire administration. While the right-wing, populist Freedom Party of Austria vigorously protested the release of these videos as mud-slinging, it had of course been their leader's willingness to sell access and privilege to a Russian oligarch (who turned out to be an actor) that tainted the party's reputations. Dirt flies in multiple directions, and in politics, it is not always obvious where it will stick.

**Notes**

1. Doron Rabinovici, "Aktion und Artikulation, Das Bestehen des Republikanischen Clubs," in Brigitte Lehmann, Doron Rabinovici, Sibylle Summer (eds.) *Von der Kunst der Nestbeschmutzung– Dokumente gegen Ressentiment and Rassismus seit 1986* (Vienna: Löcker Verlag, 2008).
2. Robert Schindel, *Der Kalte* (Berlin: Suhrkamp Verlag, 2013).
3. Ruth Beckermann, The *Waldheim Waltz*, (Austria, 2018, 93 minutes) (http://www.thewaldheimwaltz.com/en/) [accessed July 17, 2019]
4. Ruth Wodak, et. al. (eds.), *Wir sind alle unschuldige Täter!: Diskurshistorische Studien zum Nachkriegsantisemitismus* (Frankfurt am Main: Suhrkamp, 1990), 59–120.
5. Robert Schindel, *Der Kalte*, 130.
6. Georg Tidl, *Waldheim—wie es wirklich war. Geschichte einer Recherche* (Vienna: Löcker Verlag, 2015).
7. Robert Schindel, *Der Kalte*, 147.
8. Robert Schindel, *Der Kalte*, 210.
9. Robert Schindel, *Der Kalte*, 509–510.
10. Robert Schindel, *Der Kalte*, 289.
11. Brigitte Lehmann, Doron Rabinovici, Sibylle Summe (eds.), *Von der Kunst der Nestbeschmutzung – Dokumente gegen Ressentiment and Rassismus seit 1986* (Vienna, 2008).
12. Robert Schindel, *der Kalte*, 624-625.
13. Matthias Beilein, *86 und die Folgen: Robert Schindel, Robert Menasses und Doron Rabinovici im literarischen Feld Österreichs* (Berlin: Erich Schmidt Verlag, 2008), 297–325.

CROSSCURRENTS

# PURIFYING INDONESIA, PURIFYING WOMEN: THE NATIONAL COMMISSION FOR WOMEN'S RIGHTS AND THE 1965–1968 ANTI-COMMUNIST VIOLENCE

Nelly van Doorn-Harder

## Introduction

On May 29, 2006, Komnas Perempuan, the Indonesian National Commission that advocates for the rights of women, met with a delegation of nineteen women survivors of the 1965–1966 anti-Communist violence to consider their official complaint. The moment was historic: these women officially broke their silence of forty years. Between 1965 and 1968, they had been the victims of horrible acts of violence committed by other Indonesians, their neighbors, colleagues, and even friends. Participating in para-military and vigilante groups, the perpetrators had murdered between half and one million Indonesians and incarcerated more than one million. Accused of harboring Communist sympathies or being active members of the party, many of these women spent decades in jail. For forty years, the Suharto government had forbidden any mention of their plight. Their local communities, at times even their own families, had ostracized them. They had been demonized based on their direct, indirect, or alleged involvement in the Indonesian Communist Party

This material is based upon work supported by the Kroc Institute at the University of Notre Dame. Such support does not constitute endorsement by the sponsor of the views expressed in this publication. The article was written during a semester-long stay at the Center for Interdisciplinary Research (ZIF) at Bielefeld University, and made possible by a sabbatical granted by Wake Forest University, USA.

(Partei Kommunis Indonesia or PKI). The rationale for the massacres, incarceration, and silence was that Communists polluted Indonesian society and made the country impure. By virtue of their gender, women were especially susceptible to allegations of impurity, which gave their adversaries permission to rape and sexually abuse them.

Komnas Perempuan is an abbreviation that stands for Komisi Nasional Anti Kekerasan terhadap Perempuan (The National Commission against Violence against Women).[1] A government-sponsored organization, it was set up on October 15, 1998, after the collapse of the oppressive Suharto regime (1966–1998). When in the spring of 1998, during the transition period from dictatorship to democracy, large-scale communal riots erupted, many women were sexually assaulted.[2] This was not the first time such patterns of violence and sexual assault had occurred. It had been an open secret that during military operations the regime's security forces violated human rights on a staggering scale. Military personnel targeted women in places the government considered rebellious, such as Aceh, Papua, and Timor Lorosae. All through the 1990s, civil society groups insisted that the state start to accept responsibility for this particular form of gendered violence. The press and many average Indonesians observing the 1998 violence noticed that there was an eerie resemblance between what was happening at the time and previous attacks on women during the 1965–1966 events. As a result, women activists lobbied for the creation of an organization that would focus on basic human rights of women alongside the Indonesian Commission for Human Rights that is called KOMNAS HAM (Komisi Nasional Hak Asasi Manusia).

In this article, I focus on some of the strategies developed by Komnas Perempuan to address the plight of the 1965–1966 victims. By 2005, many of the women survivors were elderly and had lived most of their lives as outcasts. Their numbers were dwindling fast and there was a paucity of information about them. The main sources about their lives are interviews recorded by local organizations that try to collect the women's stories. Especially after 1998, several of such initiatives emerged all over Indonesia. Typically, they locate and interview survivors of the 1965–1966 violence to document their stories. For example, a network of organizations for Human Rights and Women's Rights in the city of Solo, Middle Java, called Koalisi Keadilan dan Pengungkapan Kebenaran (KKPK) or the Coalition for Justice and Truth Telling, collected stories about how the victims survived and dealt with the massacres. Their findings are collected in a book and a movie.[3]

The mandate of Komnas Perempuan is to report gender-based human rights abuses and create public awareness campaigns for Indonesian society. This task is not easy since it requires sustained efforts to highlight violence against women in the media. From the beginning, one of its main goals has been to change the pervasive mindset that blames the victims of sexual violence and makes their plight invisible. This attitude explains why so few cases are reported to the authorities. The consistent effort of Komnas Perempuan to inform the public has resulted in the substantial increase of the number of reports to police from 22,512 cases in 2006 to 259,150 in 2016 and 405,178 cases in 2018.[4]

Komnas Perempuan consists of multiple partner organizations (called *mitra*) that operate on the national, provincial, county, and local levels. These partners represent a large spectrum of organizations advocating and protecting women's rights. The fifteen commissioners who constitute its National Board in Jakarta are elected from across Indonesia via a rigorous vetting process that prioritizes their experience in women's rights work.

In 2005, the Komnas Perempuan leaders decided to take on the cause of the victims of the 1965–1966 events, which was a bold and controversial step. Speaking about the 1965–1966 events was taboo and more or less forbidden. Relying on their networks, Komnas Perempuan identified 122 victims of the 1965–1966 violence for their report. Their final report contradicted the dominant narrative broadcast by the Suharto regime over nearly half a century, which blamed the Communists as the sole perpetrators and villains of the violence. The Komnas Perempuan report concluded that the 1965 Tragedy remained the single most controversial problem in Indonesian society that continues to cause trauma and distrust among Indonesia's citizens. It called for the creation of spaces that allowed victims to pursue their rights to truth, justice, and healing. The organization decided not to single out individual perpetrators whose names became known via the women's official testimonies (Monitoring Report 176) but to place primary responsibility for orchestrating the violence on the State (Monitoring Report 178). It pointed to the State as the power responsible for upholding human rights and the healing of national life (Monitoring Report 185).

Officially, Komnas Perempuan is a governmental organization, created by Presidential Decree. One of its tasks is to investigate all forms of violence against women, past as well as present. Its mandate is to fulfill victims' right to truth, justice, and redress (Monitoring Report, 21). It also aims to contribute to the healing of victims (Monitoring Report 175). In the case of the 1965 victims, this mandate meant that when Komnas Perempuan accepted to investigate the women's complaint, it launched a full investigation into the events that had transpired during 1965–1968. The women's report came out five years before its counterpart, the Indonesian Commission for Human Rights (KOMNAS HAM), revisited the violence in 2012, producing an 850-page report.[5] The Komnas Perempuan report details the stories of different types of torture and abuse the women suffered. It concludes that the various ways of abusing the women constitute crimes against humanity and holds the State responsible for not acting on national reparation, healing, and the restoration of victims' rights (Monitoring Report 11–18). As I will explain shortly, several of the strategies the report mentions to address the women's trauma are not limited to the 1965–1966 victims but apply to all women victims of sexual violence.

As other survivors of atrocities, the women felt a burning need to tell their stories in order to release painful memories and trauma and to pursue a deep yearning to fulfill a deep yearning. While the violence against these victims was particularly extreme, patterns of vilifying certain groups within Indonesian society continue to this day. Since new cycles of violence against women and, for example, religious minorities are bound to happen, Komnas Perempuan leaders consider it of the highest importance to expose the underlying roots by detailing the victims' stories, as well as to help them cope and overcome trauma.

### The 1965–1966 tragedy

In spite of considerable scholarly and secondary literature, the events that led to the 65 massacres remain unclear. According to the conventional story, vividly retold by Geoffrey B. Robinson, during a coup attempt in the night of September 30 to October 1, 1965, six Indonesian army generals and one lieutenant were kidnapped and murdered (Robinson 2018). When day broke, the army led by one of the few surviving generals, future President Suharto (1966–1998), took control and issued a statement that members of the Communist Party, PKI, had been behind the murders. Shortly after, army members and civilians started to hunt down those accused of being Communists. At the time, the PKI party had around three and a half million registered members and an estimated 20 million Indonesians were affiliated with the Party via mass organizations such as the women's group Gerwani. The vast majority of the victims were ordinary people—farmers, teachers, civil servants, laborers, and artists—with no knowledge of what had transpired that September 30. As Robinson observed: "the attack on the PKI and its allies was not based on the presumption of actual complicity in a crime, but rather on the logic of *associative* guilt and the need for *collective* retribution" (Robinson 2018:7).

While the majority of killings and arrests took place in Central and East Java, as well as North Sumatra, local populations in some of the Christian dominated islands equally participated in hunting down Communists (Kolimon *et al.* 2015). Moreover, on the predominantly Hindu island of Bali numerous atrocities took place (Hobart 2014). Indonesia is a multi-religious nation with around 87% of the population professing Islam. A 1951 law had required Indonesians to identify with one of the five official religions (Muslim, Catholic, Protestant, Hindu, or Buddhist) on their identity card. However, during the 1960s, especially in rural areas, many Indonesians combined their faith with indigenous, local rituals. They were called *abangan* and often placed in contrast to practicing Muslims called *santri*. Several Muslim organizations, for example, the Muhammadiyah fought against the mixing of indigenous rituals with Islam, aiming to create a more unified, normative form of Islamic practice. When anti-Communist rhetoric increased, many *abangan* officially converted to Islam or Christianity. This move did not save them from murder or arrest when the anti-Communist purges started (Saptaningtyas and Dirdjosanjoto 2004). In the majority of Muslim areas, the most ardent participants in the purification of society were para-military groups connected to local chapters of large Muslim organizations, especially those of the Nahdlatul Ulama (NU). Nowadays, the common consensus among scholars studying this period is that the widespread and synchronized violence did not erupt spontaneously but that these groups were part of a systematic and planned military operation. This connection guaranteed that their actions would go unpunished (Crouch 1988, Kammen and McGregor 2012, Robinson 1998, Cribb 1990).

The killings, arrests, and stigmatization of all those connected with the Left created the foundation for Suharto's long-lasting authoritarian regime called the New Order that controlled Indonesia between 1966 and 1998. During that period, research and public debate about the 1965 coup and the ensuing atrocities were banned. The government created an official discourse that gave credit to the perpetrators who had been led by a self-sacrificing army (Eickhoff *et al.* 2017). Few of the victims dared to speak about their experiences openly. Indonesian poet Goenawan Mohamad captured the situation with the words "silence produces legitimacy" (Zurbuchen 2005: 49). Starting from 1984, the government mandated annual viewing of the anti-Communist government propaganda film Pengkianat G30S/PKI (The Betrayal of the September 30 Movement) in schools and on the state television channel, TVRI. According to the storyline of this film, no blood was shed but the Communist influence on society was eliminated during a legal and peaceful operation. It continues to shape the country's mindset (Emont 2015, Wargaderedia 2018).

After 1998, Indonesia transitioned from a dictatorship to a democratic nation. Liberalization of the media allowed for a hesitant public debate about what really happened during the 1965 events. A younger generation began to realize the level of brainwashing during their high school education, where 97% of the students had watched the anti-Communist film. Children and grandchildren of surviving victims and perpetrators started to ask questions and interview family members. As a result, a sense of communal guilt and a desire for accountability slowly emerged among certain groups, especially among youth linked to Muslim organizations such as the NU.

### Purifying society

Purifying society was one of the main arguments that helped the Army convince millions of Indonesians to turn on their neighbors, friends, and even family. Muslim leaders preached that Communists were rendering Indonesia impure because they were against religion. This theme still rules. In 2015, Jakarta's chief of police stated: "Islam and Communism cannot exist together" (Emont 2015). The idea that Indonesian society needed purification from anti-religious propagandists gave para-military groups connected to Muslim and other organizations permission to involve in murdering, torturing, and imprisoning at least two million Indonesian citizens.

Their actions were justified by various fatwas or legal rulings issued by groups of Muslim scholars across the nation. As early as 1957, a fatwa declared Communism *haram*, strictly forbidden. Several fatwas followed forbidding marriage and other forms of contact between Muslims and Communists (Khoemaeni 2016). Eradication of the PKI was presented as a religious duty. Some NU leaders quoted Chapter two (Al-Baqara), verse 191 of the Qur'an to "Kill them wherever you overtake them and expel them from wherever they have expelled you" (Fealy and McGregor 2012: 121). After the violence began in October 1965, a conference of religious leaders in Aceh, with a group of military officers in attendance, issued a fatwa stating that anyone who died in fighting the PKI would be considered a martyr (Salim 2008: 144–145). Communists were declared atheists and it was easily forgotten that many of the victims, similar to the majority of the population, were nominally practicing Muslims, Christians, Buddhists, or Hindus.

Due to their gender, women were specifically targeted. Shortly after the murder of the military leaders, the army started a vicious campaign of spreading rumors that women members of the PKI-related women's organization Gerwani had participated in savage attacks on the murdered generals. They had allegedly indulged in orgies with the bodies of the generals, cut off their penises, and danced around naked. According to fabricated sources, the women had polluted and desecrated the dead bodies. After dumping them in a deep well called *Lubang Buaya* (crocodile hole), the women had joined the rebels in a nightlong orgy. The goal of these stories was to impress on the general public that these women were barbaric and had broken all the rules of proper women's behavior: to be "polite, well mannered, and feminine" (Monitoring Report, 60). They were the most impure of all.

Australian researcher Annie Pohlman has argued that the new regime's ultimate goal was to portray the Communist Party as an organization that "indoctrinated women in all manner of sexually deviant behaviours" (2017: 200). The accusations that Communist women had acted with sexual license and sadistic violence placed women and women's bodies at the center of the 1965–1966 violence. It resulted in widespread sexual violence against women of all ages accused of being related to the

PKI (Pohlman and Saleh 2015, 2016, 2017:201). The stories gathered by Komnas Perempuan, Pohlman, and others show that in some cases women remained subjected to such violence for decades.

Under international pressure, by the end of the 1970s, many prisoners were released while remaining under strict supervision. However, women prisoners enjoyed little freedom as many of them continued to be raped regularly. Village heads and military leaders exploited many as personal servants and sex slaves. The general population often looked away, tolerating these acts of impunity, referencing the women's low sexual morals and the inferior position of former political prisoners. Ex-prisoners had the code ET (*eks-tahanan* or *eks-tapol*: former prisoner, or former political prisoner) stamped on their identity cards. This label meant that their movements were restricted and that they did not have the basic rights Indonesians enjoy. They could not live among the general population and were not allowed to travel freely. Their children inherited this status, and even their grandchildren could be banned from working in public service, the military, and the press. Most jobs were closed to them, and their children were denied education. As Katharine McGregor observed: "Children and grandchildren of those killed and of political prisoners in Indonesia were stigmatized in society as being of an 'unclean environment'"(2013: 353). Decades later, some grandchildren could be denied permission to register for the pilgrimage to Mecca on the premise of being "unclean" (McGregor 2013: 354).

### Women's impurity

In her famous work *Purity and Danger,* Mary Douglas observed that defilement occurs in relation to a systematic ordering of ideas (2002:42). When groups or individuals do not respect the conventional boundaries set by society, the threat to the social equilibrium creates forms of pollutions (Kristeva 2000: 21) Religious systems in particular provide frameworks for beliefs and practices relating to purity as symbolic expressions (Katz 2005: 109). A large part of the Indonesian population still considers Communism as a disturbance and threat to the social order, especially since in the mind of the majority it is joined with atheism. Within religions, upright moral behavior often connects to a high level of purity of the individuals involved. A 2013 Pew Study Report found that, especially, in Southeast Asia, more than nine-in-ten Muslims believe that an individual's morality is linked to belief in God, which means that Communists are of low morals.[6] Denial to go on the Hajj is one example of how family connection to an immoral, polluting entity not only prevents full participation in society, but for a Muslim, can become an obstacle for religious practice as well.

Considering these Islamic teachings in conjunction with local culture, these women suffered from a triple layer of impurity, in body as well as in spirit. The first layer was the label of Communism; the second was the general population's assumption that victims of sexual violations are impure; and the third layer derives from cultural beliefs and religious teachings about the inborn nature of a woman. Within this frame of reference, the female political prisoners subjected to rape were impure on all three accounts. Across Indonesia, a tenacious prejudice prevails that blames the victim. Many reports published by Komnas Perempuan document the mechanisms by which victims of rape are blamed for their predicament. In many cases a woman is accused of inviting the attack, even though their attackers are usually in positions of power vis-à-vis the victim. In the case of the former women prisoners, their supervisors abused their authority to violate them with impunity after release from prison.[7] Members of their village, neighborhood, and even their own family would not interfere assuming that somehow the women had invited their own violations. When women prisoners shared their ordeal with their closest family, they would sometimes be asked to leave the home of their parents or siblings. There are even cases where a husband and wife both survived years of detention, that the husband refused to accept what had happened to his wife and cast her out as "a whore and immoral" (Monitoring Report 157).

The deep-seated prejudices and expectations about women's proper behavior are based on an amalgam of religious teachings as well as local and cultural beliefs and practices. Local culture buttresses the opinion of women as unclean and of lesser spiritual value. Although gender culture is not static across the many islands and cultures of Indonesia, classical texts that remain influential until today teach that a woman has to comply with her husband's wishes and sacrifice herself for the well-being of her husband and children (Smith-Hefner 2019).

Sexual slander about Gerwani women ignored religious affiliations but arose from the deep-seated ideas about a woman's essential or innate nature (*kodrat*). Many of these ideas derived from classical Javanese texts written at medieval royal courts that are still being referenced in the Islamic handbooks taught at Indonesian Qur'an schools. They portray a woman as weak and submissive; her salvation depends on the husband's spirituality (van Doorn-Harder 2006: 41–42) According to Muslim feminist scholar Faqihuddin Abdul Kodir, who teaches at the Islamic University in Cirebon and is one of the founders of the Fahmina Institute, an Indonesian NGO working on gender, democracy, and pluralism from an Islamic perspective: in Javanese culture, "women's virtue was judged entirely by how much pleasure they brought to their husbands' lives ... a woman belongs to her husband. She must surrender her entire life to her husband's desires" (van Doorn-Harder 2006: 108–109). Local Islamic teachings elaborate on these convictions. For example, texts that are still widely used in the traditional Qur'an schools state that God granted men superiority to women in marriage, economics, politics, and knowledge (Anwar 2018:218). Some quote the Islamic Tradition (Hadith), according to which the Prophet Muhammad once said, "women are men's prisoners" (Anwar 2018: 221).

Following Islamic Jurisprudence, a woman is impure when menstruating or experiencing other forms of bleeding that need ritual washing. According to various Islamic interpretations, a state of bodily purity is imperative for ritual participation. External purity reflects internal purity and relates to one's moral agency (Katz 2005). States of minor pollution occur after bodily functions such as using the bathroom, and need to be addressed by performing the *wudū'*, the ritual washing Muslims perform several times a day before ritual prayers. While the *wudū'* involves running water over one's limbs, menstruation causes major pollution and requires a more comprehensive washing ritual. However, based on certain *Hadith* texts, Muslim scholars have stressed that the *wudū'* ritual also points at inner cleansing and washes away sin and purifies the body for the Day of Judgment (Katz 2005: 117–119). The exterior purification of the body thus points to its internal purity (Katz 2005: 121). According to Marion H. Katz, "The *wudū'* ritual thus becomes a concentrated exercise in moral regeneration, culminating with a reaffirmation of one's faith" (Katz 2005: 125).

Due to their alleged corrupted and decadent nature paired with an "atheist" mind and a body defiled by rape, Communist women were perpetually in a state of pollution. Rape sometimes caused additional bleeding, causing further pollution. The goal of sexually violating them was to destroy physical integrity and any sense of morality. They were made worthless in their own eyes, as well as to society and its institutions, including religious institutions. While not all communities refused these women participation in worship, some Muslims certainly assumed that they should not do so. Furthermore, intense feelings of shame and guilt prevented the women from attempting to participate in public life, including religion. The label of impurity kept them from performing the primary method of purification, ritual washing. This could have severe consequences, as in some cases, decades later, grandchildren could be prohibited from the Hajj, a ritual that can only be performed in a state of purity. Some Muslim leaders even teach that an impure state prevents entry into heaven.

One of the survivors, *Ibu Astuti,* describes this state of limbo as follows:

> They tortured us, the women PKI, with sexual abuse, it was sexual abuse against us. They attacked us by destroying our morals, our dignity as women. As women, we became worthless because they destroyed [our dignity], trod on it, we were worthless after that. We were made worthless! People thought that [about us], society thought that, that's what it was like! Normally, we'd be worth 100%, but things turned a complete 180 degrees. We weren't valuable to other people any more (Pohlman and Saleh 2015: 70–71).

The fabricated discourse about the Communist women that the army created during the 1960s was the preamble to what later became official conservative gender ideology of the Suharto regime. Indonesian feminists called the ideology "state ibuism," "state motherhood." It taught that women existed to serve husband and nation. It rested on traditional ideas of womanhood, upholding the ideal that the family was the basis of state and society in which women were subordinate to men. During the 1950s, PKI-related Gerwani women had been the most active in advocating the rights of women within the marriage, at the workplace, and when seeking education. Even Suharto's predecessor, Sukarno, struggled with Gerwani women forcing them to subordinate their agenda that focused on empowering women to the nationalist project (Smith-Hefner 2019: 85). By vilifying Gerwani members, Suharto also succeeded in linking the idea of women's political activism with sexual and moral depravity (Wieringa 2002: 281, Pohlman and Saleh 2012, 2017). This move not just rendered these women unworthy members of society but also brought other women organizations in line. Suharto's regime ended in 1998, but nowadays, the label of "Communist" continues to be a powerful tool to discredit women activists.

However, during the 1990s, the writings of influential Muslim feminists such as Riffat Hassan and Amina Wadud became available in Indonesia, and religiously based feminist ideas percolated through civil activist groups into newly founded women's studies departments at universities across Indonesia. Muslim feminists started to study primary and secondary texts to learn about human rights, gender equality, and the influence of religion and culture. They reinterpreted the Qur'an and other authoritative texts to empower women. Christian feminists did the same with the Bible. These ideas and activities created a growing cohort of scholar activists who realized the importance of exposing the gender aspects of the anti-Communist atrocities. It was impossible to understand "the violence itself and its legacy for Indonesia," without taking into account the role of sex and gender (Pohlman and Saleh 2015, 2017: 205).

Using different channels such as op-eds in the press, classes at Islamic universities, and civil rights organizations, Muslim feminists started to develop alternative interpretations of the Qur'an and the tradition to counter prejudiced teachings of women's secondary nature (Anwar 2018, van Doorn-Harder 2006). Women's agency is derived from concepts such as becoming a servant of God (*'abd*) and the practice of correct doctrine and worship (*ibādah*). Women's independence comes from observing virtues such as sincerity *(ikhlās)*, God-consciousness (*taqwā*), and righteousness (*sālihāt*) (Anwar 2018: 227). This focus on practice and worship requires the performance of ritual prayers five times a day, including the ritual washing or *wudū'*. To activists, it appeared unthinkable that any woman would be denied participation in the ritual worship based on misogynist ideas of purity.

#### Accountability and responsibility

After the fall of Suharto, several initiatives emerged to encourage national healing and to demand that the numerous human rights violations during the New Order regime be revisited (Kimura 2015: 77). On March 15, 2000, the president of Indonesia and long-time chair of the NU Abdurrahman Wahid issued a personal apology for the murders of 1965–1968 (Eickhoff *et al.* 2017: 449). However, his apology was not translated into concrete initiatives. Those responsible for the violence have never been prosecuted, let alone punished. Army leadership has prevented any legal recourse for the victims. The Indonesian equivalent of the South African Truth and Reconciliation Commission that held public hearings about human rights abuses failed. In 2004, a body called The Commission for Truth and Reconciliation was launched, but despite the reality that "pressures for transitional justice have appeared both externally and internally," the Commission was abolished (Kimura 2015: 90). When in 2014 Joko "Jokowi" Widodo became president, activists hoped that there would be serious attempts to redress past wrongs and again requested an apology from the state. During an official ceremony, which commemorated the slain generals, Jokowi explained why this was not an option: "Apologize to whom?" he asked, "Who should forgive whom when both sides claim to be victims?" (Emont 2015).

One of the pressing questions facing the Komnas Perempuan leaders remains what type of solutions can satisfy the victims of the anti-Communist purge. Part of Indonesia's younger generation is asking similar questions. A sense of intergenerational guilt confronts them with issues of fairness and equity (Baumeister *et al.* 1994: 251). Although they are not directly responsible for the atrocities, their mindsets were shaped by prejudices that allowed the acts of aggression to take place and could make it possible that similar episodes of violence happen again. Their proof was the 1998 riots. They are also drawing a direct line to recent trends of decreased religious tolerance that have led to lethal attacks on groups labeled as deviant, such as the Ahmadiyyah and Shi'ite Muslims (McGregor 2013: 358). Communists were called "deviant" (*sesat*) as well. Whether or not members of their family were involved in the 1965–1966 Tragedy, the cloud of an unaddressed history of violence hangs over the lives of the younger generations.

Philosopher Iris Young has suggested that in cases of historical injustice in which a state refuses any form of accountability or responsibility and when many of the injured parties are no longer alive, it is preferable to apply what she calls the "social connection model of responsibility"

(Young 2013: 178). This model does not assign blame or fault but aims for social reformation and policy reform. Similarly, anthropologist John Borneman defines reconciliation as a departure from violence (Borneman 2011:61). But in current-day Indonesia, violence against women continues to saturate society. Therefore, this reconciliation has not yet happened. Truly diminishing various forms of violence against women would require a social revolution. Minimally, it calls for changes to mindsets that are biased against women, an exercise that will take several generations.

Young's social connection model is helpful to understand the basic approach of Komnas Perempuan, which seeks to create new social structures and to restore a woman's dignity on the basis of women's experience. Helping women regain their dignity and self-worth is the first objective, with changes to prevailing ideas about women's intrinsic secondary status to follow from that. First, Komnas Perempuan seeks to empower the victim and to encourage victims to support each other. But it also looks for opportunities to translate local ways into changes for women's rights in the legal system. Local cultures and conditions provide resources for the oppressed. Despite their focus on victims, they do not ignore state institutions and political actors, whose impunity encourages continuity and repetition. For example, in the border area between Malaysia and the province of Kalimantan, a Komnas-related group found that the local army leaders were the main facilitators in trafficking young girls.[8]

The women victims of 1965–1966 were allowed to tell their stories for the first time in any detail in the Komnas Perempuan report of 2007. Their testimonies and memories provided tools for an entire new generation of Indonesians struggling with their status as members of an implicated community. Memory and storytelling follows the model suggested by John Borneman, which outlines four modes of accountability in order to refigure the losses: (1) retribution, (2) restitution/ compensation, (3) performative redress (for example, apologies), and (4) rites of commemoration (Borneman 2011: 3). In Indonesia, performative address and rites of commemoration remain the most feasible. However, every year the organization mentions newly found information about "unsolved impunity" in its annual reports. Komnas Perempuan also has worked with various governmental agencies to guarantee medical care for the victims. It refers to the 1965–1966 data as it continues building programs to prevent torture.[9]

Concerning the 1965–1966 women victims, Komnas Perempuan's main strategy seeks a form of rehabilitation that is not just based on justice or monetary compensation, but involves the rehabilitation of the women's humanity. Supported by a cohort of Indonesian Muslim, Christian, and other feminists, Komnas Perempuan seeks to lift the stains of shame and impurity by challenging conventional discourses and prejudices about women. For this exercise, they refer to feminist works that deconstruct and reinterpret traditional misogynist texts. The reeducation of the public, of men and women, is one of their express goals. In the end, it is not society that purifies the women, but the women purify each other as well as themselves. They regain their voice by supporting each other. They find the strength to hold up a mirror to society, in which the perpetrators see themselves, realizing that they are impure, rather than the victims they defiled. Nina Nurmila, Professor of Gender and Islamic Studies at the State Islamic University (UIN) in Bandung, and one of the Komnas Perempuan commissioners expressed this new reality in a meeting with me on June 22, 2019: "Of course, the victims are always pure. It is the perpetrator who is impure!"

In their testimony, many of women who fell victim to the anti-Communist purges speak to their intense experience of shame, which forced them to avoid the main streets of their villages and neighborhoods and to walk through the fields instead of having to deal with hateful looks or gossip from the neighborhood. Regaining their voice was a breakthrough they did not imagine possible during their lifetime. Their autobiographical accounts accelerate and continue to appear.[10] Their voices are finally heard, most powerfully attested by the Dialita Women's Choir organized by survivors of 1965 repression, who were awarded the Gwangju Prize for Human Rights for their contributions to "showing the path of reconciliation and healing through music" in May 2019 (Dipa 2019). They received this prize mostly for helping to remove the stigma of impurity from these victims of 1965. Their personal plight for women is being translated into campaigns for greater justice and accountability and provides impetus to educate a younger generation in finding new understandings of the rights of women on the basis of religious texts.

## Notes

1. http://www.komnasperempuan.or.id/
2. https://web.archive.org/web/20000920073842/http://www.serve.com/inside/digest/dig86.htm
3. For more information about the book and the movie see: https://www.spekham.org/menemukan-kembali-indonesia/ [accessed June 24, 2019].
4. Komnas Perempuan, "Labirin kekerasan terhadap perempuan: dari perkosaan berkelompok hingga femisida (*femicide*), alarm bagi Negara untuk bertindak tepat. Catatan kekerasan terhadap Perempuan tahun 2016. Komnas report. (Jakarta, March 7, 2017) 10.
5. Only the executive summary is available: Ringkasan eksekutif: Hasil Penyelidikan Tim Ad Hoc Penyelidikan Pelanggaran Ham Yang Berat Peristiwa 1965–1966. http://lama.elsam.or.id/downloads/861153_Ringkasan_Eksekutif_Penyelidikan_Peristiwa_65.pdf
6. The World's Muslims: Religion, Politics and Society. https://www.pewforum.org/2013/04/30/the-worlds-muslims-religion-politics-society-morality/ [accessed June 24, 2019].
7. C.F. Komnas Perempuan 2005, "Sistem Peradilan Pidana Terpadu Yang Berkeadilan Jender dalam Penangan Kasus Kekerasaan Terhadap Perempuan," Jakarta.
8. Interview with Ose, Interim Director of the K3JHAM group in Semarang, June 11, 2016.
9. Interview Komnas Perempuan Vice-Chair Yunianti Chuzaifa and Commissioner Mariana Amir ud-Din, June 24, 2019.
10. https://www.spekham.org/menemukan-kembali-indonesia/ and https://tirto.id/ikhtiar-kebenaran-dan-rekonsiliasi-kasus-65-di-solo-dan-palu-dczY [accessed June 24, 2019].

## Works Cited

Anwar, Etin, 2018, A Genealogy of Islamic Feminism. Pattern and Change in Indonesia, London & New York: Routledge.

Baumeister, Roy F., Arlene M. Stillwell, and Todd F. Heatherton, 1994, "Guilt: An Interpersonal Approach," Psychological Bulletin **115**(2), pp. 243–67.

Borneman, John, 2011, Political Crime and Memory of Loss, Bloomington and Indianapolis: Indiana University Press.

Cribb, R, ed., 1990, The Indonesian Killings of 1965–1966: Studies from Java and Bali, Clayton, Victoria: Centre of Southeast Asian Studies, Monash University, Centre of Southeast Asian Studies, Monash University.

Crouch, Harold, 1988, The Army and Politics in Indonesia, Ithaca, NY: Cornell University Press.

Dipa, Arya, 2019, "1965 survivors choir 'Dialita' awarded Gwangju human rights award," The Jakarta Post, May 19, 2019. https://www.thejakartapost.com/news/2019/05/19/1965-survivors-choir-dialita-awarded-gwangju-human-rights-award.html

van Doorn-Harder, Pieternella, 2006, Women Shaping Islam. Reading the Qur'an in Indonesia, Urbana and Chicago: University of Illinois Press.

Douglas, Mary, 2002, Purity and Danger: An Analysis of the Concepts of Pollution and Taboo, London and New York: Routledge.

Eickhoff, Martijn, Gerry van Klinken, and Geoffrey Robinson, 2017, "1965 Today: Living with the Indonesian Massacres," Journal of Genocide Research **19**(4), pp. 449–64.

Emont, John, 2015, "The Propaganda Precursor to the 'Act of Killing," The New Yorker. https://www.newyorker.com/news/news-desk/the-propaganda-precursor-to-the-act-of-killing

Fealy, G., and K. McGregor, 2012, "East Java and the Role of Nahdlatul Ulama in the 1965-66 Anti-communist Violence," in D. Kammen, K. McGregor, eds., 2012, The Contours of Mass Violence in Indonesia 1965–1968, Singapore: NUS Press, pp. 104–30.

Hobart, Angela, 2014, "Retrieving the Tragic Dead in Bali. Regenerating Rituals after the 1965-1966 Massacre," Indonesia and the Malay World **42**(124), pp. 307–36.

Kammen, D, and K. McGregor , eds. 2012. The Contours of Mass Violence in Indonesia 1965–1968. Singapore: NUS Press.

Katz, Marion H., 2005, "The Study of Islamic Ritual and the Meaning of *Wudū*," Der Islam **82**, pp. 106–45.

Khoemaeni, Syamsul Anwar, 2016, "Ulama Sempat Haramkan Muslim Nikah degan Keluarga PKI," https://news.okezone.com/read/2016/06/01/337/1403607/ulama-sempat-haramkan-muslim-nikah-dengan-keluarga-pki

Kimura, Ehito, 2015, "The Struggle for Justice and Reconciliation in Post-Suharto Indonesia," Southeast Asian Studies **4**(1), pp. 73–93.

Kolimon Mery, Wetangterah Liliya, Campbell-Nelson Karen, Lindsey Jennifer, eds. 2015. Forbidden Memories. Women's Experiences of 1965 in Eastern Indonesia. Clayton, Vic: Monash University Publishing.

Komnas, HAM, 2012, "Ringkasan eksekutif: Hasil Penyelidikan Tim Ad Hoc Penyelidikan Pelanaggaran Ham Yang Berat Peristiwa 1965–1966".

Kristeva Julia. 2000. The Sense and Non-Sense of Revolt. The Power and Limits of Psychoanalysis. New York, NY: Columbia University Press.

McGregor K. 2013, "Memory Studies and Human Rights in Indonesia," Asian Studies Review **37**(3), pp. 350–61.

Perempuan Komnas. 2005. Sistem Peradilan Pidana Terpadu Yang Berkeadilan Jender dalam Penangan Kasus Kekerasaan Terhadap Perempuan. Komnas Perempuan: Jakarta.

Perempuan Komnas. 2007a. Kejahatan terhadap Kemanusiaan Berbasis Jender: Mendengarkan Suara Perempuan Korban Peristiwa 1965. Jakarta: Komnas Perempuan.

Perempuan Komnas. 2007b. Women's Human Rights Monitoring Report. Gender-Based Crimes Against Humanity. Listening to the Voices of Women Survivors. Jakarta: Komnas Perempuan.

Pohlman, Annie, and Ismail Saleh, 2012, "The birth of the New Order state in Indonesia: sexual politics and nationalism," Journal of Women's History **15**(1), pp. 70–91.

Pohlman, Annie, and Ismail Saleh, 2015, Women, Sexual Violence and the Indonesian Killings of 1965–1966, London: Routledge.

Pohlman, Annie, and Ismail Saleh, 2016, "Janda PKI: Stigma and Sexual Violence against Communist Widows Following the 1965–1966 Massacres in Indonesia," Indonesia and the Malay World **44**(128), pp. 68–83.

Pohlman, Annie, and Ismail Saleh, 2017, "The Spectre of Communist women, Sexual Violence and Citizenship in Indonesia," Sexualities **20**(1–2), pp. 196–211.

Robinson, Geoffrey, 1998, The Dark Side of Paradise: Political Violence in Bali, Ithaca, NY: Cornell University Press.

Robinson, Geoffrey, 2018, The Killing Season. A History of the Indonesian Massacres, Princeton: Princeton University Press, pp. 1965–6.

Salim, Arskal, 2008, Challenging the Secular State: The Islamization of Law in Modern Indonesia, Honolulu: University of Hawaii Press.

Saptaningtyas, Haryani, and Pradjarta Dirdjosanjoto, 2004, "Religious Conversion in Central Java. Struggling for space in two local communities," in Kumar Giri, Ananta, van van Harskamp, Anton, and Salemink, Oscar, eds., The Development of Religion. The Religion of Development, Delft: Eburon, pp. 153–62.

Smith-Hefner, Nancy J., 2019, Islamizing Intimacies. Youth, Sexuality, and Gender in Contemporary Indonesia, Hawai'i: University of Hawai'i Press.

Wargaderedia, Arzia Tivany, 2018, "The Creators of 'G30S/PKI," Reflect on the Film's Impact Three Decades Later. The anti-communist movie continues to shape minds 34 years after its release," October 2, 2018 https://www.vice.com/en_asia/article/3kepn8/the-creators-of-g30spki-reflect-on-the-impact-of-indonesias-most-watched-propaganda-film

Wieringa, S. E., 2002, Sexual Politics in Indonesia, New York: Palgrave MacMillan.

Young, Marion Iris, 2013, Responsibility for Justice, Oxford: Oxford University Press.

Zurbuchen, Mary S, ed., 2005, Beginning to Remember: The Past in the Indonesian Present, Singapore: Singapore University Press.

# BOOK

## THE BIBLE'S GREATEST MEME?

### *The Book of Exodus: A Biography*. By Joel S. Baden, Princeton, NJ: Princeton University Press, 2019. xv + 215 pp. $26.95.

No serious reader, student, or teacher of the Bible can fail to see that the Book of Exodus is the key to the Hebrew Bible-Old Testament and perhaps to all of Sacred Scripture. Genesis has many more appealing folkloric tales and mythic moments, but Exodus is absolutely indispensable. Here, we meet God as the Lord of history, the force that created and saved his own people, the Israelites, and bound himself to them forever in a solemn, all-encompassing Covenant. Baden is a professor of Hebrew Bible at Yale Divinity School, and his work is part of the Princeton Press's "Lives of Great Religious Books"; but he focuses less on the text of Exodus (or Shemot) than on the astonishing power of the Exodus story to shape and enrich religious traditions not just in Judaism, but in a bewildering variety of Christian churches.

At the heart of the narrative is something like a complete historical blank. Exodus 12.37 claims that the Israelites had 600,000 foot soldiers, which translates into a minimum total population or two million; and scholars are agreed that there is no archeological or written evidence of such a mighty horde having lived in Egypt or survived for forty years in the Sinai desert. And was Moses himself an actual personage or a fictional hero? What to make of his Egyptian name and his supposed royal upbringing? Why did Yahweh want to kill Moses (in Ex. 4.24) shortly after the sublime theophany on Mt. Sinai/Horeb? How is it that God's grandest spokesman had a speech defect and was told to let his highly flawed brother Aaron occasionally take his place? Was Moses really barred from entering the Promised Land, after all his years of toil and travail, simply because he struck a rock to make it gush water (Num. 20.11-12) instead of just bidding it to do so?

As for the mass departure from Egypt, the most one can say is that a group of runaway Hebrew slaves may have escaped from Egypt (at some time in the thirteenth-century BCE?) and made their way into Canaan, where they joined up with some distant tribal kin. And the confusion thickens when we consider the incompatible or contradictory elements in Exodus supplied by the J, P, and E strands of tradition that have been woven together. (E.g., were there seven plagues or ten?) The eating of matzah is an essential feature of Passover, but it turns to have nothing to do with the Exodus, only connected to it by the invented detail that the fleeing Israelites had no time to bake normal leavened bread.

And the problems go on, but no matter, because in the Exodus God both makes his tremendous intervention in the life of Israel and establishes the core of Judaism forever. Once again, historical realism has to admit that Moses himself could no more have delivered the vast body of specific legal material in the Torah (much of which refers to conditions in a future settled country, rather than the wasteland of Sinai) than he could have described his own mysterious death and burial in Deuteronomy 34). And finally, there are the painful issues of the death of the Egyptian first-born and the army of Pharaoh, which we'll get to later (Baden doesn't deal with them).

The point is that, historical disputes aside, Pesach joins all Jews celebrating it into an organic symbiosis with a primordial liberation (whatever it may have exactly been) and all past generations who have ever liturgically participated in it. Unlike formal, clerically led synagogue services, Passover is a home-based, democratic affair, with a unique focus on children. The Seder replaces the obsolete (since the destruction of the Temple in 70 CE) Passover sacrifice. Baden calls the Passover Seder "an act of commiseration and of communal redemption," whose relevance never fades.

And, of course, it flowed into the life blood of Christianity. Jesus is at once the new Moses (especially in the Gospel of Matthew, in the Sermon on the Mount, say), the people of Israel itself, who went down into Egypt and survived the Pharaoh's (Herod's) murderous intent, and the sacrificial victim (Jesus as the Lamb of God in John's Gospel). With Paul in the lead, Christians abandoned much of the Law beyond the Ten Commandments, but maintained the notion of themselves as "a chosen race, a royal priesthood, a holy nation, God's own people" (1 Pet 2.10), participants in a new, but everlasting Covenant. Unfortunately, though he defended the Jews in Romans, in First Thessalonians Paul sounded the dismal theme of supersessionism, writing of "the Jews, who killed both the Lord Jesus and the prophets, and drove us out, and displease God and oppose all men by hindering us from speaking to the Gentiles that they may be saved" (2.14-16). Jesus was the fulfillment of the Law and the Prophets, as shown by the appearance of Moses and Elijah in the Transfiguration (Mt. 17.1-2).

Protestants like Luther and Calvin seized on Exodus, identifying the pope with Pharaoh and themselves with the oppressed Hebrews. Inevitably, various bands of Christian sectarian refugees, like the Pilgrim Fathers, copied the pattern, with the Atlantic serving as a giant replica of the Red Sea, and the native Americans all too often re-envisioned as Canaanites, whose defeat and annihilation were dictated by the ethnic-cleansing "ban" of Deuteronomy 7 and other ferocious passages. Not just the Puritans, but even secular minds like Benjamin Franklin and Thomas Jefferson welcomed the image of the Exodus, which they saw, however, as an act of political self-emancipation rather than providential rescue. The Abolitionists constantly preached about Exodus, and many hailed Abraham Lincoln as a modern-day Moses. George Washington had once been accorded such laurels, but he lived and died a slave-owner. Joseph Smith viewed the Mormons as the New Israel, and Brigham Young led a huge exodus to Utah. Like the Pilgrims, the Mormons had outdone the Israelites by traveling farther and by a more than dangerous route than their predecessors'.

In the twentieth century, the Civil Rights Movement and liberation theology made much of Exodus motifs, although blacks, like the poor in Latin America, Christian American Indians, or Christian Dalits in India, had the problem of being trapped in the land of their taskmasters, with no Promised Land to venture to. Baden gives fairly extensive and strongly sympathetic coverage to the work of Gustavo Gutierrez and James Cone, whose pages are understandably lit up with anger at the contemporary houses of bondage.

Meanwhile, the Exodus story, for all its dramatic tension and exhilarating climax, has more than a few ironies, which have been often overlooked. First of all, the once-enslaved Hebrews were freed—but took on a new status as slaves of the Lord (*'ebed* in Hebrew means both servant and slave). And, worse yet, the Covenant Code (like the New Testament) never condemns the institution of slavery, though it aims at partly mitigating the lot of Hebrew slaves. And weirdly enough, for all its majesty and fascination, the Book of Exodus contains two long sections, chapters 25-31 and 35-41 about the ark, the table, the lampstand, the altars, the tabernacle, and various other cultic accouterments that have to rank among the most boring in the Bible. (Baden unapologetically calls them "excruciating.")

But what about the victims of the Exodus? There is an oft-quoted passage from the Talmud (Megillah 10b and Sanhedrin 39b (tr. Uri L'Tzedek) to the effect that God rebuked the "ministering angels [who] wished to utter the song [of praise] to celebrate the successful Israelite crossing of the Red Sea, by "saying: My handiwork [the Egyptians] are drowning in the sea, and would you utter song before me?" That's touching, but it ignores all the dead first-born of "the maidservant(s) who sit behind the mill" (Ex. 11.5) or the other non-royal Egyptians who died (or lost their cattle or jewelry) to make the Israelites' victory as spectacular as possible.

The Exodus might be called a miracle, but it was also a political revolution, and revolutions tend to be bloody. And believers who take Exodus as a tale of utopian triumph have to face the disconcerting fact that immediately after crossing the Red Sea the first Exodus generation began to "murmur" against God and Moses and proved in the end to be such immoral, idolatrous failures that all of them, except Caleb and Joshua, were denied entry into Canaan and left their bones to bleach in the wilderness.

In any case, the revolutionary potency of the Exodus has insured its continued vitality. Baden concludes on an ecumenical note, with particular stress on liberation theology, and subordinating, as he has all along, strictly textual and scholarly arguments—as seen, for example, in Richard Elliott Friedman's *The Exodus: How It Happened and Why It Matters* (2017)—to life in the here and now.

> Liberation theology reveals that the power of the Exodus story can be expressed in both faith and practice, in theological inquiry and in lived action. The premises that liberation theology highlights are those that have been central to Exodus: oppression and redemption, the work of the divine in human history, and the omnipresent hope for a better future.

Baden has a lively, clear, accessible style, and he presumes little or no prior knowledge of his subject. Even when treating complicated matters, such as Philo of Alexandria's attempt to read the Torah allegorically as a sort of treatise on natural law, he's easy to follow and even-handed. (Princeton University Press, however, should have published this book, which would be ideal for Bible study courses, in a larger format, with a longer index.) But it is altogether a persuasive, sensitive, and pleasurable performance.

—*Peter Heinegg*

# BOOK

## CONDEMNING THE CONGREGATION

***The Immoral Majority: Why Evangelicals Choose Political Power over Christian Values.*** **By Ben Howe, New York, NY: Broadside Books, 2019. xiii +265 pp. $26.99**

Ben Howe was raised both solidly Republican and devoutly evangelical. Born in Dallas, he moved with his family to Lynchburg, Va., where his father, Thomas Howe, did graduate work in Biblical Studies at Liberty University, worked for the Rev. Jerry Falwell Sr., and belonged to his Thomas Road Baptist Church in Lynchburg, before moving on to become a professor at Southern Evangelical Seminary in Matthews, N.C. Ben founded a video production company, was a Tea Party activist, and blogged for the conservative website Redstate, before being fired for airing his anti-Trump views. His book is a fierce, evangelically orthodox tirade (appropriately published by "Broadside Books") at the vast bloc of evangelical voters, who constitute 26% of the American electorate, and roughly 80% of whom fanatically support Trump.

This is an astonishing phenomenon. It has been studied in depth, for example, by Frances Fitzgerald in *The Evangelicals* (2017), and it will be explored by historians, sociologists, and political scientists for years to come. Howe is not a scholar or academic. This is a tormented *cri de coeur at* what he sees as the trashing of the Christian virtues and values he grew up believing in and thought were firmly entrenched in his own community of faith and the thousands of others around the country.

It has to be said from the outset that, despite his honesty, earnestness, and self-critical spirit, Howe has a narrow focus (he says next to nothing about evangelical perspectives on foreign policy, racism, the environment, misogyny, crime, drugs, etc.), and he's consistently naive in exaggerating the sins of the left (where, if anywhere, would he find the leftist American equivalents of Rush Limbaugh, Alex Jones, Richard Spencer, Sean Hannity, or even the Reverends Jerry Falwell, Jr. and Franklin Graham?—Bill Maher on a bad day, maybe; but Stephen Colbert? Rachel Maddow? Dana Millbank? Maureen Dowd?) Howe seems to be still licking the verbal wounds inflicted on him personally by (unnamed) anti-religious, leftist hard-liners. But his case has merit, precisely because its strictures come from an unimpeachable, straight-shooting insider who takes no pleasure in the indictment he has drawn up.

Without specifying a particular origin or date for the evangelical movement in America, Howe says that "for decades" evangelicals have been called to reestablish Christian values as "the central doctrine of their political motivations." That's a vague formula, but he goes on to say:

> Above all else we were tasked with growing God's kingdom, preserving His creation, helping the poor, and loving the downtrodden. Despite evangelical leaders' *talk* of character, their followers have the inverse priorities. That these leaders can't recognize that it's their hypocritical actions that have led to this gap between abstract ideals and real-life priorities is precisely reflective of how they've chosen to misuse the mantle of leadership. By directly defying their stated desire, ignoring the character of Donald Trump, and creating a "Christian'" culture that has become divisively self-interested and bitterly self-righteous, these leaders have taught their flocks to value the things of the world, rather than the things of Christ.

Among these leaders is Dr. Robert Jeffress (one has to wonder about the intellectual seriousness of all those televangelist doctorates), the pastor of Howe's childhood First Baptist Church in Dallas, which has a congregation of some 13,000 members and a vast radio and TV outreach. Jeffress has gone on the record as saying that the last kind of president he'd prefer is one who governed by the principles of the Sermon on the Mount. He thinks the country needs an amoral, Machiavellian strong man not a saint. Mission acomplished.

This is just one of whole series of rationales that prominent evanglicals have devised to paper over Trump's contempt for Christian, or any other kind of real, morality. Some of them compare Trump to King Cyrus of Persia, who, unbeknownst to himself, was God's instrument for enabling the Jews to return from their exile in Babylon. And if he's done some, well, brutal things, then perhaps Trump resembles Joshua, whom God assigned the task of —as it were—draining the swamp of Canaan. Evangelicals now look at behavior that stirred their outrage and indignation when it occurred in Clinton's White House as no problem at all.

Trump hasn't offered his clerical cheerleaders any help by his ludicrous ways of talking about religion, for example, calling the eucharist "drinking my little wine, having my little cracker," saying he had never asked God's forgivenesss for anything, or remarking that, "'I don't bring God into that picture (his moral lapses, if any). I don't." But people like Franklin Graham have never been at a loss to champion Trump's hostility to Islam or to provide biblically flavored nostrums for the unease of believers worried by Trump's triumphant immorality: "King David committed adultery and murder ... There's no perfect person." So there.

The character issue could be seen as the hub of a wheel with many policy spokes; but this part of the book is sketched in rather hazily. It's clear that the Trump's Weltanschauung, like his private life, is ruthlessly selfish, egomaniacal, and composed of a thousand falsehoods. Howe condemns all this, as he must; but he never spells out what a wide-ranging evangelical political platform might look like, apart from a few generalities. No abortion, to be sure, and some forms or other of "charity" wherever possible. But what about the nitty-gritty questions: How many immigrants and refugees to admit? (In "Why People Hate Religion" [NYTimes, Aug. 30, 2019], Timothy Egan cites a Pew Report from May 24, 2018, that by a ratio of 68 to 25 percent American evangelicals say the United States has no obligation at all to accept refugees, how to attack income inequality? How to tackle global warming? Racism? The gun bloodbath? Poverty and oppression locally and globally?) If, as Reinhold Niebuhr said, individuals may be thoroughly moral, but society cannot, how to draw up a Christian masterplan, if only as a counter-thrust to Trumpianism and the fanatical Trump base?

Still loyal to his old political connections, Howe has warm words about George W. Bush, without mentioning the apocalyptic horrors launched, and still ongoing, by his mendacious quest for Saddam Hussein's non-existent WMDs. Howe showers praise on Mick Mulvaney for one miniature moment of decency: He tried to convince hardline Republicans that Iowa's unspeakable Steve King, who said that, "For everyone who's a valedictorian, there's another 100 out there who weigh 130 pounds—and they've got calves the size of cantaloupes because they're hauling 75 pounds of marijuana across the desert," was being overly harsh (not to mention politically counter-productive). But Howe completely ignores Mulvaney's shift from calling Trump "a terrible human being" to serving as the President's shameless propagandist, plus a host of highly shady dealings catalogued on Wikipedia and elsewhere.

Mulvaney, in fact, serves as a perfect illustration of Howe's central thesis that "*the* issue with Trump is less about what *he* does and more about what *other people* do on his behalf or in opposition to him." Putting aside the question of the feeble whataboutism in that last phrase, surely Howe disagrees with Mulvaney's aiming to cut grants for Meals on Wheels or his refusal in 2018 to meet any lobbyists unless they first contributed to his congressional campaign.

In any event, Mulvaney (who happens to be a Catholic) is just one instance of the reigning Republican ethic of take no prisoners and anything goes, as illustrated, say, by the language of conservative columnist Kurt Schlichter, who rejoices in the new "conservative corps that is willing to mock the members of that motley collection of pompous, inept, lying jerks we call the Democrat Party and its media catamite corps."

Howe laments the sowing of such division, and he calls out evangelicals for their relentless promoting of it. And he repents for the fierce partisan style of his own earlier blogging days. Incensed by liberal attacks on police officer Darren WIlson for the shooting of Michael Brown in Ferguson, Missouri (even after local authorities and the Justice Dept. found Wilson acted in self-defense), Howe defiantly declares, "Give me a gun. Put me in Darren Wilson's shoes. I'd have shot Mike Brown right in his face." Howe regrets having said that, and he clearly wishes his former comrades-in-religio-political arms would acknowledge their excesses, past and present.

But once again he fails to appreciate the depth of what a consistent Christian might call the age-old national sins that lie at the root of our current political conflicts. He casually blames the "modern Trumpist conservative right" on nothing more ominous than "the polarized Obama years, the excesses of political correctness culture, (and) the hyperbolic liberal claim that most things are motivated by racial hate." He can't see its more extensive roots in the larger national moral failures of 400 years of Indian genocide, slavery, and racial injustice, of entrenched plutocracy and sexism, of capitalist plunder and working-class exploitation, of imperialism and the psychotic arms race, and of speciesism and ecological destruction. These are structural sins, not simple flaws that reading and approving the indignation expressed in a well-intentioned tract like this can erase.

Howe's title is, of course, a reversal of Jerry Falwell, Sr.'s "moral majority." But he doesn't seem to understand just how ethically vile Falwell's thinking was. He says, "I disliked much of Falwell Sr.'s approach, but I never doubted whether he believed what he was saying, even if I often thought he sold it poorly." That poor salesmanship presumably refers to Falwell's notorious dictum that least "some of the burden" for 9/11 must be laid at the feet of abortionists, pagans, feminists, gays and lesbians, the ACLU, etc. But there's worse than that here. Howe should have read some of Falwell's repulsive screeds, such as *Listen, America!* (1981), where he blasts the evils of government welfare programs and offers a folksy true-life parable by way of a solution: He was once given two Irish setters, with a note about what kind of meat they liked. Realizing that feeding them that way would cost a fortune (this was presumably before he attained his final net worth of $10 million), he bought them a "big bag of brown nuggets" instead. The dogs went on a four-day hunger strike, but eventually caved. Moral of the story: The poor can get by on cheap puppy chow.

The intermingling of religion and politics, in America and elsewhere, has always been a knotty problem, and Howe can be pardoned if, given his unsophisticated evangelical convictions, he can't come up with a fully coherent analysis. He voted for neither Trump nor Clinton, but he won't say for whom. He stresses simplistically that in the end all you have to do is vote your conscience. (But consciences can be well-informed or uninformed or completely misled.) "The important choice was never between Donald Trump and Hillary Clinton" (never?)—"the important choice was between-self-interest and the idolization of 'winning' versus loving God and one another. And ...

far too many evangelicals have chosen the former over the latter."

A noble sentiment, perhaps, but it doesn't get us very far. In the face of all the warring positions that what is pretty much a binary presidential-election choice did and will soon involve, which lever should a Christian pull? (Is obliged to pull?) To what extent can one just render the things of Caesar to Caesar (whether by opting for the status quo or following rational self-interest)? What is the moral status on not voting at all? (The New Testament naturally says nothing about representative government or any civic duties except obedience to imperial authority, and the primitive Church lived in eager expectation of the Parousia.)

At any rate, there can't be much disputing about whether Trumplandia is unchristian, like the larger nationalistic, narcissistic, xenophobic region to which it belongs. And insofar as Howe has struck a few honest, heartfelt blows against it, he deserves our appreciation.

—*Peter Heinegg*

# BOOK

## SUMMA ANTI-THEOLOGICA

***This Life: Secular Faith and Spiritual Freedom*. By Martin Hägglund (New York, NY: Pantheon Books, 2019), 450pp. $29.95.**

Despite the fairly widespread readership of the New Atheists (Dawkins, Hitchens, Harris, et al.), they have also been widely panned in Academe as crude, arrogant, and superficial. In any case, the debate over their position has been muddled by the fact that most of them, save for Daniel Dennett, are nonphilosophers, and their opponents have frequently been slow-moving targets like televangelists and right-wing Evangelicals. Martin Hägglund isn't, technically speaking, a philosopher either, but a Swedish-born professor of Comparative Literature and Humanities at Yale, who has not only read his way through the corpus of western European philosophy, but doesn't hesitate to quarrel with major figures like Spinoza, Hegel, Kierkegaard, or Marx, when he catches them in inconsistencies or failing to take their own positions to the logical limit. His book is a dense, passionate, fiercely abstract case for atheism, but it scores its points more against religion as traditionally defined than as concretely lived.

The key word in Hägglund's argument is "secular," meaning of this world, finite, evanescent, death-bound, fragile (and, he might have added, tragic). Religion for him comprises every kind of doomed attempt to escape the secular. He defines it as "any form of belief in an eternal being or an eternity beyond being, either in the form of timeless repose (such as nirvana, a transcendent God, or an immanent, divine Nature.") Cue John Lennon singing "Imagine."

Hägglund goes to work, deconstructing and devastating any mode of such notions, because on close inspection they're unthinkable, incoherent, and futile exercises in mental gymnastics. If we were somehow freed from time, we'd have no shape or identity, no past, present, or future, no story, no goals, no relationships, and on and on. We'd be trapped in a shapeless, colorless ether that could neither be perceived, grasped, or moved in any direction. If we could completely achieve the Stoic ideal of *apathia* (total painlessness and emotional quiescence) or Buddhist nirvana, we would no longer be human.

So, are religious people deceiving themselves, or just hopelessly sloppy thinkers? (What would a daily schedule in Paradise look like?) Hägglund suggests believers don't literally mean their blissful term "forever"; it's just a very long time or on and on. (How could you talk meaningfully about something you've never experienced and can't really explain?) He doesn't bother to address the juridically impossible problem of eternal Hell for time-bound evil acts. And Hägglund seems to ignore the curious paucity of details supplied about the afterlife in the New Testament, which has much to say about Judgment and separating the righteous and wicked, but precious little about what happens next. Is it an accident that St. Paul, who was never at a loss for words, wound up describing the next world so vaguely: "What no eye has seen, nor ear heard, nor the heart of man conceived, what God has prepared for those who love him" (1 Cor. 2.9—and half that line was borrowed from Is. 64.4).

There are, of course, graphic images of heaven as a city made of jewels, the New Jerusalem, at the end of the Book of Revelation; and the Qur'an paints sensuous pictures of Jannah; but these are mythic fantasies and tell us nothing about Hägglund's chief preoccupation: time. It's easy enough to depict scenes of thunderous celebration (the Hallelujah chorus), but in the only world we know these moments are always followed by the return to gray everydayness. So, perhaps believers are a kind of absurdists, who refuse to accept the world and life as they are, and chase after transcendent visions that they know, at some level anyhow, are blind leaps of faith. More to the point, they ignore rigid theological constructs (the geometry of faith) and embrace its poetry instead. In other words, believers probably care a lot less about eternity than Hägglund thinks they do.

In classic existentialist fashion, Hägglund says the secular person must have "secular faith," in the sense for striving for personal and social justice, for the best life possible, with no hard and fixed system to shape his or her decisions, no Almighty Lawgiver, and certainly no guarantee of success. He speaks disparagingly of religious types who claim to possess a timeless pre-established code, with rewards and punishments meted out to those who obey or disobey it.

But is that the actual moral psychology of believers (like passengers going all out for frequent-flyer miles?)? Couldn't one (don't many people) fulfill what they hold to be a sacred law out of love or perform a mitzvah for the sheer joy of it—all the while recognizing that moral acts have a rational validity as well? And when it comes to moral goodness, whether ordinary or heroic, how much do motivations and rationales matter? In a text otherwise devoid of concrete examples, Hägglund devotes a long section to the last years of Martin Luther King, Jr. and his evolution from a scripturally based prophetic preacher to a humanistic revolutionary. Reflecting on King's speech, given just before his assassination, about not getting to the promised land, Hägglund observes:

> King's vision of the promised land is not a vision of eternal life–not a vision of the new Jerusalem–but a vision of what we the people can achieve, a vision of the new Memphis. Because it is a vision of collective emancipation that can become a reality only through our generational efforts, it does not project a timeless eternity where we will all come together as one. Rather, King's

vision of the new Memphis is committed to a temporal future that we ourselves may not live to see. Like King, we may not get there. Yet we can act on behalf of the new Memphis, we can own it as our spiritual cause, we can make it our creed through our deeds.

Actually, it looks as if throughout his career, King's choice of the ministry had always been more pragmatic than pious. But once again how much does that matter? The most striking thing about King's message, more than a half-century after his death, might well be how far away we still are from that promised, however construed. Hägglund stresses that, going back to his graduate school days, King's favorite thinker was always Hegel; and Hegel demanded that "we ourselves produce the communal norms that we instigate through our practices." By contrast, "religious forms of faith ... ultimately disown our spiritual freedom." Could be, but when King famously quoted Amos 5:24, "Let justice roll down like waters, and righteousness like an ever-flowing stream" in his "I have a dream speech," did that verse make King's appeal in any way derivative or less his own? Regardless of whether one takes Amos to be a divine spokesman or just a brilliant writer, his words add weight.

There's a strong utopian drive to Hägglund's thinking, and he likes to envision his fellow secularists coalescing in a community of "democratic socialism," where the measure of wealth is "socially available free time" (creative opportunity, not just a dose of distracting r. and r. before the next round in one version or other of the privately owned dark satanic mills of capitalism). In Hägglund's ideal state, the "pursuit of labor" is strictly determined, not by profit, but by the classic formula of "from each according to her ability [and] to each according to her need."

Hägglund won't accept mere liberal reforms and improvements (even radical redistribution of wealth) to the capitalist societies we're the prisoners of. But isn't he being too ideologically pure here? Wouldn't the (let's face it) far-fetched prospect of a fiercely progressive income tax, a massive expansion of the welfare state, and the payment of reparations to historically oppressed minorities constitute a stunning blow to capitalism? He dismisses most of the changes wrought by advanced technology and robotics as "not *worth* anything in itself under capitalism, since value can be generated only through the exploitation of living labor time" (through either automation-caused unemployment or slavish "socially necessary labor").

But has anything like this ever come into being? Hägglund naturally has nothing but contempt for the pseudo-Marxist communist states of the twentieth century. One wonders, might the primitive Christian community in Jerusalem (Acts 2.45-46) or even a Buddhist or Christian monastery qualify as partial models of "democratic socialism"? With their strict schedules and harsh asceticism, medieval monasteries may or may not have been forerunners of modern capitalism, but they provided at least a few individuals, like Thomas Aquinas (1225-1274) the leisure to engage in creative endeavors for their own community and the world beyond.

By the way, we know that Aquinas never claimed that God's existence could be rationally proved, only that there were (five) ways of "demonstrating," that is, pointing to it; and he had the habit of prefacing his philosophical assertions with the phrase *videtur quod non*, that is, this seems to be mistaken, my opponents seem to be right. In our time, the celebrated Christian novelist, Marilynne Robinson, has harshly scolded atheists. At a symposium on "Arguing Belief and Unbelief," held at Skidmore College in September, 2015, she said: "I am religious *not* because I find rationalist refutations of religion to be illogical, uninformed, and ill-considered—though I do." As James Wood pointed out in his review of *This Life* (in *The New Yorker*, May 20, 2019), that thrust hardly does justice to a long line of atheistic authors. Wood starts with Pliny (but he might just a well have cited Lucretius) and invokes Montaigne and James Baldwin (Hume and Nietzsche would obviously have made the team as well). They were certainly not "uninformed."

Robinson hasn't done her homework, but then she's an artist, not a deeply learned, polyglot anti-theologian like Hägglund. There's no refuting his claim that believers often talk and act in ways that contradict their bedrock belief in eternity and the promise of the resurrection (as seen, for instance, in St. Augustine's grieving over the death of Monica, and Martin Luther's heartbroken grief over the death of his daughter Katharina). Are believers, Hägglund might have asked, less visibly crushed and desolate than atheists at funerals? How many Christians could sincerely echo the Pauline dilemma: "I am hard pressed between the two. My desire is to depart and be with Christ, But to remain in the flesh is more necessary on your account" (Phil. 1:24-25)? Like many saints, Muhammad may have declared (29:64) that, compared with eternity, this life was but a brief "diversion," but he, and they, lived it with what Hägglund would have to admit looks like tremendous amount of "secular" attention and energy.

But then once again, given the unremitting lack of "socially available free time" (something likely to pain both tenured Yale professors and working-class stiffs), given the endlessly vulnerable hopes and schemes we all nurture, the failed and successful interactions with others, the kaleidoscopic vagaries and vicissitudes of everyday life, is there any necessary reason why the lives of believers and unbelievers should *feel* so different, even for "advanced" practitioners of either *Weltanschauung*? Catholic hagiography loves to recreate the last days of St. Francis Xavier, who died at the age of 46, utterly exhausted and feverish, on the island of Shangchuan, some ten miles off the southern coast of China, staring off longingly at the grand unknown kingdom he would never live to enter, much less evangelize.

Hägglund would maintain that Xavier must have taken comfort in his faith-based assurance that this setback was all a part of salvation history, and in one way or another God would see to the salvation of the Chinese.

From Hägglund's perspective, then, Francis must have died happily. Maybe so, but the folk-tale version of the event has Xavier dying of something like a broken heart. By the same token, faith in God's absolute loving redemptive power should theoretically mean that believers are permanently buoyed up by the conviction that, "The eternal God is thy refuge, and underneath are the everlasting arms" (Dt. 33:27), but generations of mystics and devout believers of every kind have reported the grim phenomenon known as "the dark night of soul," where they effectively repeat Jesus' cry, "My God, my God, why has thou forsaken me?" (Mt. 27:46).

None of this is meant to erase the enormous, age-old differences between theism and atheism. Both writers may have been brilliant young Frenchmen with dramatic visions and vivid styles, but there's no way to conflate Pascal's *Pensées* and Camus' *Myth of Sisyphus*. Yet Pascal's *libertin* is a kind of troubled secularist, and the universe he wrestles with is just as vast and inscrutable as Martin Hägglund's. Can we call them brothers beneath the skin? They both can be torn by conflicting moral imperatives. (They also have an unfortunate tendency to be too self-obsessed to worry about the fate of animals and non-human nature.) Hägglund welcomes finitude, while the religious person dreams of escaping it, though all accounts of that escape are of necessity metaphorical (e.g., nirvana comes from the Sanskrit term for extinguishing a flame; the Latin word for heaven, *caelum* also means "sky").

Hägglund doesn't provide any specific scenarios for the realization of his ultimate ideal, "socially available free time." Yet one can't help miss the fact that he himself has personally enjoyed a juicy chunk of it through his membership (2009-2012) in the Harvard Society of Fellows, a scholarly Land of Cockaigne, where three dozen pre- or brand new Ph.D.s are paid to engage in any kind of intellectual activity they please, with no teaching duties and no publish-or-perish deadlines.

Hägglund is perfectly aware that this blissful interlude is made possible by Harvard's nearly 40 billion dollar endowment, in other words naked capitalism. And he may feel more than a little twinge of guilt over this. But he has boldly proceeded to trace out an ideological blueprint of a world that might have room for more and altogether different "Societies of Fellows," unbelieving part-time versions of the Abbey of Thélème for every sort of person. But it's significant that Hägglund's deconstruction of otherworldly theology (as opposed to homely biblical-religious practice) is a lot clearer and sharper than his map of "democratic socialism." Perhaps he should spend some time reading the foundational documents of the great religious orders —the Benedictines, Franciscans, or Jesuits, say. Though sorely beset nowadays by scandals and slumping vocations and burdened with unusable ascetic peculiarities (compulsory celibacy, etc.), these organizations did enjoy many centuries of successful experimentation and just might offer some interesting insights for an apostle of secularism who, like the old Catholic founders, realizes that the world is in very bad shape and begging for radical institutional innovation. Atheists to the rescue!

*—Peter Heinegg*

# BOOK

## DISFELLOWSHIPPED!

***Leaving the Witness: Exiting a Religion and Finding a Life.***
**By Amber Scorah, New York, NY: Viking, 2019. 279 pp. $28.**

The (sometimes sudden) gain or loss of faith, the religious or philosophical aha-moment, is one of the great recurrent themes of western literature. On the positive side of the ledger, we immediately think of St. Paul, Augustine, Francis of Assisi, Pascal, Rousseau (who got his dramatic political prophetic calling en route to Vincennes to visit Diderot in prison) or John Stuart Mill (saved from the sterility of Utilitarianism by the beauty and warmth of Wordsworth's poetry). On the negative side, once the topic of atheism ceased to be taboo, books from ex-believers began tumbling from the press: Renan, Nietzsche, Edmund Gosse, Joyce, Mary McCarthy, Fawn Brodie, et al.

Though the dramatic models of Paul and Augustine, fusing a complex evolutionary process into an instant crystallization or bolt from the theological blue (or empty heavens) always had a undeniable seductive appeal, the simple fact seems to be that erecting or exploding a body of belief always takes time. But once the person involved realizes the immensity of the change that has taken place, he or she may well feel, in one way or another, thunderstruck.

Amber Scorah started out as a Jehovah's Witness in Vancouver (throughout the book she is stingy with dates), indoctrinated not by her badly matched and lukewarmly practicing parents, but by her devout grandmother. She followed all the rules, crazy as many of them seemed, sitting through long, boring services in Kingdom Hall, avoiding outsiders, not celebrating birthdays, Christmas, or Easter, refusing blood transfusions, obeying the inerrant dictates of the patriarchal "Governing Body," and buying into the absolute veracity of the Bible and the approaching apocalyptic Armageddon that will destroy all non-Witnesses. College education is forbidden, and so Scorah never got past high school.

Her story begins when, stuck in a loveless, lifeless marriage, she looks for adventure by becoming a missionary to China (legally forbidden, of course). She first spent three years or so in Taiwan, learning Mandarin and preparing herself for her underground assault on godless communism. Her earliest efforts were floundering, given her still imperfect Chinese and the vast cultural distance between the Watchtower and Shanghai (or anywhere else in China), and eventually (since she has to support herself), she got into producing and appearing in podcasts teaching Mandarin and various puzzling features of China to foreigners. All the while she had to disguise her proselytizing as harmless friendly contacts (which is what they mostly were) with random Chinese persons. She made no converts (her message was hopelessly foreign to them), but a few friends and engaged in modest amounts of touristic discovery, which were all the more stimulating after her hopelessly drab and narrow earlier life. In the meantime, the figure of her (unnamed) husband and theoretical fellow missionary is practically invisible and non-existent.

Her life takes on a radical shift when she starts exchanging emails with "Jonathan," an LA-based fan of her "Dear Amber" podcasts, who proceeds to mix flirtation with an extended tutorial on the cultic qualities of the Jehovah's Witnesses. This is, needless to say, an inappropriate relationship, but Scorah had already violated the JW code by engaging in a teenage premarital affair back in Vancouver. She gradually sees that he's right about the oppressive irrationality of her religion and even flies to California to meet and have a predictable, brief affair with him (he eventually dumps her).

Now that she has seen the light, Scorah takes the fateful step of publicly announcing her apostasy to the Shanghai Witnesses, for which she is ruthlessly "disfellowshipped," leaving her severed for good from "family members, all of my friends, my future, my past, my life with friends and family in it, my faith, my certainty, my hope, my purpose in life." Physically speaking, her devastation is less than total because she still has "a rented apartment, a job, in China, people at my work who knew I existed and would notice if I disappeared, at least," a handful of personal items, plus "my health, a couple thousand renminbi in a shared bank account, people who listened to my podcast."

One more thing that Scorah didn't have—and still doesn't have, apparently—is knowledge of Barbara Grizzuti Harrison's *Visions of Glory: A History and a Memory of the Jehovah's Witnesses* (1978), an oddly structured but vivid, painful, and deeply personal account of life as a child and adolescent in the JW, along with a survey of their history. The book would have taught Scorah everything she learned from Jonathan's emails and warned her about all the intellectual and psychological damage she was doing to herself by remaining in the Witnesses.

A year after being disfellowshipped (cults seem instinctively tone-deaf to the English language), Scorah flew back, not to Vancouver, but to New York where, untrained and physically handicapped as she tried to start off a new life. There she suffered an unspeakable tragedy when her four-month-old son died in his first day in day care from what sounds like an act of criminal neglect. Then, she gave birth to a daughter, who survives and brings her joy, though she dedicates the book to her dead son, Karl. Scorah ends her story on a characteristic note of lyrical agnosticism:

> The question of my son–the mystery of his death, his whereabouts–remains without answer.
>
> And so I ask the questions of life: What force grew this little child? How did that spine and those limbs form themselves from nothing

> inside of me? Why did I have the power to make him, but not to bring him back? What are the things he saw on this planet so beautiful? Why did his eyes look at me the way they did? Where did love like this come from? How, in the face of so much pain, was there also beauty?
>
> This alchemy of life, this magical planet, they bewilder me, they awe me. But no understanding comes, any more than it did to any other human who walked this hard land, feeling entitled to explanations where there are none. I have called a truce with the unknown, and I am learning to live with the disquiet. I do not attempt to pray to a God who will not answer.

Most people, it seems likely, don't think, much less analyze, but feel their way into and out of religion. Scorah responded to her doubt and religious restlessness not by studying the bizarre spiritual world she had grown up in or the alternative secular one she was entering, but by striking out in search of adventure and even, to a certain degree, danger. When it came time to break with the JW, she did so through a series of actions—flying alone to Jonathan in LA, openly admitting her adultery and her apostasy to the harsh, unforgiving community elders, and surviving on her own. She experienced all that as a nano-version of a key Witnesses' tenet and metaphor: an apocalypse. So what, if, as she wisecracks, "The closest thing to the Four Horsemen was a Trojan condom wrapper on the floor"? She would never be the same again and would always be defined by her rebellion.

Naive and artless as she comes across, Secah is nonetheless a natural storyteller. She has a sharp eye, a quick pace, and a keen sense of everything going on around her—not least because she led such a blinkered constricted existence before her awakening. Given all this intensity, one can forgive her amateurish narrative lapses: We get no sense whatsoever of her husband and her marriage, the psychology of her personal piety, or the group of New York friends and supporters whom she ultimately managed to find a home with, including the person(s?) who fathered her children. With luck, her gifts will grow and mature, and she'll be able to shed a sharper, more nuanced light on her spiritual past—and future.

—*Peter Heinegg*

# BOOK

***Faces of Muhammad: Western Perceptions of the Prophet of Islam from the Middle Ages to Today.*** By **John V. Tolan. Princeton, NJ: Princeton University Press, 2019. xii + 309 pp. $29.95.**

There are many stories told about, and words attributed to, the great religious founders, the Buddha, say, and Jesus, and Muhammad, although very little of all this material is verifiable history in the strict sense. Professor Tolan teaches history at the University of Nantes; but in any case his subject is not the actual person of Muhammad, but "Mahomet," the construct or fantasy or caricature created by western writers from roughly the twelfth to the twenty-first century. It's safe to say that no other major religious figure has been as distorted and vilified as the Prophet—though there are some important exceptions to this wrongheaded record. But Tolan's dense, briskly moving summary (which could well have been far longer) tells us not about Islam, but the various cultural agendas of Europeans reacting to what they thought Islam was or looking to gain some sort of polemical mileage out of their misguided notions.

For medieval crusade chroniclers, "Mahomet" was a golden idol, a false god worshiped by the "Saracens" (= Arabs, but connected by a folk etymology to Sarah), a term Muslims never used to describe themselves. Or else, he was a master heretic who seduced Christians into the toils of a false faith, and was thus consigned by Dante to the ninth trench of Hell in a gory scene that Tolan oddly skims over. Such gross distortions lingered on for ages, but in the sixteenth century Miguel Servet (1509 or 1511–1553), better known as Michael Servetus, like later "Unitarians," drew upon the Qur'an for arguments against the Trinity, only to be burned at the stake in Geneva for his troubles.

As wars between Catholics and Protestants began to tear Europe apart, some critics cited the tolerant view of religious diversity in the Qur'an and the Ottoman Empire. In the seventeenth and eighteenth centuries, anticlerical writers praised Muhammad as a "reformer who abolished the privileges of a corrupt and superstitious clergy." In the eighteenth and nineteenth centuries, Muhammad was sometimes treated as "a sort of Arab national hero, bringing law, religion, and glory to his people." Voltaire (1694–1778) tried to have it both ways. In *Fanaticism, or Mahomet the Prophet: A Tragedy* (1736), he uses the old cliché of Muhammad the imposter as a stalking horse to attack targets closer to home. But in his huge *Essay on the Manners and Thinking of the Nations* (begun in 1756), he takes a much more broad-minded view, comparing him favorably to Alexander the Great, calling him not a fanatic, but an "enthusiast." "As a conqueror, legislator, monarch, and pontiff, he played the greatest role that can be played on earth in the eyes of the common people." Note the culminating swipe, which Voltaire couldn't resist. To be sure, Voltaire prefers Confucius to Muhammad because Confucius was a purely rational sage who foreswore the Prophet's modes of worldly power, just as he prefers the Chinese to the Arabs because he thought they were more "civilized." Still, though parts of the Qur'an may be contradictory, absurd, or confused, other passages are "sublime." All things considered, Voltaire considers Muhammad a great man and a hero. Figures as disparate as Goethe, Napoleon, and Thomas Carlyle would strongly agree.

Eventually, as time went on, the work of scholars, translators, and other western experts, sometimes unfairly tarred as "Orientalists," made it possible to arrive at a fairer assessment of Muhammad. In the English-speaking world, ground-working was done when George Sale produced a serviceable, unbiased translation of the Qur'an (1734), with a prefix validating the Prophet as a righteous enemy of superstition and overweening clerical privilege. Before Sale, in 1671 Henry Stubbe, who knew no Arabic and read most Islamic documents in Latin translation, published his *Originall & Progress of Mahometanism* with a preface that hails Muhammad as "a religious reformer, beloved and admired ruler, and sage legislator." Stubbe was the very first European non-Muslim to take such a positive stance; and once again, this vision of the Prophet provided ammunition for contemporary anticlerical writers, like the Irish Deist (and near-namesake of the author) John Tolan, against the power and pretensions of the Church of England. Over two centuries later, Nietzsche, though Tolan ignores him, had high praise for the "virility" of Islamic culture (e.g., in *The Antichrist*, 66), as opposed to the sickly "decadence" of Christianity.

Tolan's book is essentially a catalog, largely of items that could be labeled curiosities, because so many of them were based on ignorance, ill will, or sheer fantasy, which range from the utterly silly to the fascinating. A typical example of the former is the account by the poet (and wandering monk) John Lydgate, who, at some point between 1410 and 1450, passed on the canard that Muhammad had trained two doves to pick grains of wheat out of his ears, so he could claim he was being given messages from God:

> On his shuldres wer ofte tymes seyn,
> Whan he to folkes shewed his presence,
> Milk whit dowes, which that piked greyn
> Out of his eris; affermyng in sentence
> Thei cam be grace of goostli (spiritual) influence
> Hym to visite, to shewe and specifie
> He was the prophete that called was Messie.

Muhammad a false Messiah! This was standard medieval fare; and Tolan offers many samples of it. European

Islamophobes loved to mock the endlessly repeated fable that Muhammad's coffin was miraculously suspended in mid-air. On the other hand, the intense curiosity Europeans felt about the Ottoman Empire in the sixteenth century could feed on all kinds of reports from people who had actually been to that exotic, threatening world as visitors or escaped prisoners. One author known as George of Hungary wrote a book about "the Rites and Customs of the Turks" after twenty years of imprisonment in Istanbul. It was written sometime after the middle of the fifteenth century and was still going strong in 1530, when it inspired Martin Luther, of all people, to write an introduction to it, where he said:

> The religion of the Turks or Mahomet is far more splendid in ceremonies ... than ours, even including that of the religious or all the clerics. The modesty and simplicity of their food, clothing, dwellings, and everything else, as well as the fasts, prayers, and common gatherings of the people ... are nowhere seeen among us ... Furthermore, which of our monks, be it a Carthusian ... or a Benedictine, is not put to shame by the miraculous and wondrous abstinence and discipline among their religious? Not even true Christians, not Christ himself, not the apostles or prophets ever exhibited so great a display. This is the reason why many persons so easily depart from faith in Christ for Mahomet and adhere to it so tenaciously.

Almost as surprising, if only at first glance, is Tolan's choice for the key Enlightenment and therefore modern, western witness to, and reappraiser of, Muhammad's greatness: Edward Gibbon, in the fifth and last volume of his *History of the Decline and Fall of the Roman Empire* (1788). Gibbon, of course, treated much of religion and Christian doctrine in particular with (barely) veiled contempt; but he had an accurate knowledge of Patristic theology. As Tolan says, he put down seventh-century Byzantine Christianity as "a degenerate faith in need of a radical reformer"—and Muhammad filled the bill. Gibbon's portrait of Muhammad in Chapter 50 is altogether lyrical:

> Qualifications of the prophet.
>
> According to the tradition of his companions, Mahomet ... was distinguished by the beauty of his person, an outward gift which is seldom despised, except by those to whom it has been refused. Before he spoke, the orator engaged on his side the affections of a public or private audience. They applauded his commanding presence, his majestic aspect, his piercing eye, his gracious smile, his flowing beard, his countenance that painted every sensation of the soul, and his gestures that enforced each expression of the tongue. In the familiar offices of life he scrupulously adhered to the grave and ceremonious politeness of his country: his respectful attention to the rich and powerful was dignified by his condescension and affability to the poorest citizens of Mecca: the frankness of his

manner concealed the artifice of his views; and the habits of courtesy were imputed to personal friendship or universal benevolence. His memory was capacious and retentive; his wit easy and social; his imagination sublime; his judgment clear, rapid, and decisive. He possessed the courage both of thought and action; and, although his designs might gradually expand with his success, the first idea which he entertained of his divine mission bears the stamp of an original and superior genius.

The stage was now set for the serious learned assessments of future centuries. For a handy survey of this sort, see *The Norton Anthology of World Religions: Islam* (Eds. Jane Dammen McAuliffe and Jack Miles, 2017). Tolan's latest good citizen in the realm of Islamic studies is Montgomery Watt (1909-2006), who was both an academic and an Anglican priest. But then again, Tolan is not primarily interested in the *real* Muhammad, but in the thought processes concerning him of mostly ill-informed and bigoted outsiders. Yet even an empirically impeccable biography of the Prophet (could that be had) wouldn't satisfy believers, any more than the most scrupulously fair account of the "historical Jesus" (were *that* ever obtainable) could be made to rhyme with the Nicene Creed. And even the most dedicated and flexible ecumenists sooner or later run up against irremovable differences with their dialog partners. But, following Tolan's lead in *Faces of Muhammad,* they —and fair-minded readers everywhere —are bound to be encouraged by how far we have come (in principle anyway) from the ignorant misreadings, empty fabrications, and mean-spirited demonizing of the past, As Horace (and Kant) would urge us, *sapere aude!*

—*Peter Heinegg*

# CONTRIBUTORS

**Roger Fayet** is Director of the Swiss Institute for Art Research (SIK-ISEA) in Zurich and Lausanne and Adjunct Professor (PD) of Art History at the University of Zurich, Switzerland. He wrote *Reinigungen: Vom Abfall der Moderne zum Kompost der Nachmoderne* (Wien: Passagen Verlag, 2003), and edited *Verlangen nach Reinheit oder Lust auf Schmutz? Gestaltungskonzepte zwischen rein und unrein* (Wien: Passagen Verlag, 2003). He is the author of *Die Logik des Museums. Beiträge zur Museologie* (Baden: Hier & Jetzt Verlag, 2015) and editor of *Im Land der Dinge. Museologische Erkundungen* (Baden: Hier & Jetzt, 2005) and *Anatomie des Bösen. Ein Schnitt durch Körper, Moral und Geschichte* (Baden: Hier & Jetzt, 2008). From 2009 to 2015, he was President of ICOM Switzerland, and from 2011 to 2017, he was Vice-chair of the International Association of Research Institute in the History of Art (RIHA).

roger.fayet@sik-isea.ch

**Iris Hermann** is Professor of Contemporary German Literature at Otto-Friedrich-Universität Bamberg. She published *Die Ästhetik des Schmerzes in Literatur, Musik und Psychoanalyse* (Heidelberg 2006) and *Fährmann sein. Robert Schindels Poetik des Übersetzen* (Göttingen 2012). Her most recent essays include, "Mit einer Frage beginnt die Nacht: Gedichte und Prosaminiaturen Ilse Aichingers aus den 1950er Jahren." In: *Treibhaus. Jahrbuch für die Literatur der fünfziger Jahre*. Edited by Günter Häntzschel, Sven Hanuschek und Ulrike Leuschner, Band 6 (2010), and "Zur Kategorie der Empathie im literarischen Text: Überlegungen zu Maxim Billers Roman Die Tochter." In: *Sprache und Literatur*. 106 41. Jg. 2010 (2), S. 96–111. Her research interests include Jewish literature, contemporary literature, literature and emotion.

iris.hermann@uni-bamberg.de

**Meinolf Schumacher** is Professor of Medieval German Literature at Bielefeld University. His doctoral thesis *Sündenschmutz und Herzensreinheit* (Munich 1996) surveys the metaphoric language of impurity and purification in medieval Latin and German literature. His most recent article examines the symbolism of hand washing in Christian liturgy and medieval literature: "Lavabo in innocentia manus meas. . .Zwischen Schuldanerkennung und Schuldabwehr: Händewaschen im christlichen Kult" (2019). He is a fellow of the ZiF research group *'Felix culpa'? – Guilt as Culturally Productive Force*.

meinolf.schumacher@uni-bielefeld.de

**Nelly van Doorn-Harder** is Professor of Religious Studies at Wake Forest University and also teaches at the Vrije Universiteit Amsterdam. Her work focuses on issues of gender, leadership, interfaith engagement, and freedom of religion. Her latest edited volumes are *Kebebasan Beragama Di Tingkat Akar Rumput*. With Mega Hedayati. *Religious Freedom at the Grassroots: An Analysis of Case Studies* (2018), and *Copts in Context: Negotiating Tradition, Transition and Modernity* (2017). She is a fellow of the ZiF research group *'Felix culpa'? – Guilt as Culturally Productive Force*, where she focuses on gendered guilt, shame, and purity in Indonesia.

vandoopa@wfu.edu

**Katharina von Kellenbach** is Professor of Religious Studies at St. Mary's College of Maryland, USA, and author of *Anti-Judaism in Feminist Religious Writings* (Oxford University Press, 1994), and *The Mark of Cain: Guilt and Denial in the Lives of Nazi Perpetrators* (Oxford University Press, 2013). She is Co-editor of *Von Gott reden im Land der Täter: Theologische Stimmen der dritten Generation nach der Shoah* (Wissenschaftliche Buchgesellschaft, 2001) and *Mit Blick auf die Täter* (Gütersloher Verlagshaus, 2006). Since October 2018, she serves as co-convenor of the ZiF research group *'Felix Culpa'? Guilt as Culturally Productive Force* at Bielefeld University and is writing her new book *Composting Guilt: The Purification of Memory after Atrocity* (Oxford University Press, 2019).

kvonkellenbach@smcm.edu

**Deborah Williger** received her PhD in agricultural sciences with special expertise in milk cows from the university Kiel and her Master of Science in International Agricultural Development from the TU Berlin. She worked in Germany, Austria, and India, including as estate manager of an organic farm, consultant for rural agricultural development, in product management, as well as to control genetically modified feed for life stock. Switching careers, she received her MA in Jewish Theology from the University of Potsdam and currently serves as lecturer and member of the Board of the Institute of Theological Zoology, ITZ, at the Philosophisch-Theologische Hochschule Münster.

Dvora@t-online.de

**Peter Heinegg** was born in Brooklyn, spent seven years in Jesuit seminaries, and received a B.A. in English from Fordham University and a Ph.D. in Comparative Literature from Harvard University. He has taught at Harvard, Queens College, C.U.N.Y. and at Union College in Schenectady, where he is a professor of English and Comparative Literature. He is the author of numerous translations of books on religion and theology, of book reviews, and volumes of collected essays on religion and contemporary culture. He has contributed to the Christianity section of the Norton Anthology of World Religion. His special interests include the Bible, anti-Semitism, and the history of belief and unbelief in 19th century Europe.

peterheinegg@hotmail.com

www.ingramcontent.com/pod-product-compliance
Lightning Source LLC
LaVergne TN
LVHW052347100826
845147LV00012B/771

*9781469667201*